Big Philosophy
for
Little Kids

An Affective Curriculum While Learning to Write

Frank Marrero, M.A.T.

ISBN 978-0-9673265-7-3

for further information see:
frankmarrero.com/big-philosophy-for-little-kids/index
amazon.com/author/frankmarrero

Sherrill Teague wins "Pi Day", 3/14/2010.
They never forget how to use 3.14.

BUSTED!

Enjoyment accelerates learning.

Praise for the Affective Effectiveness of
Big Philosophy for Little Kids

(and *The Royal Games* — the predecessor to *Big Philosophy for Little Kids*)

Scholars

I am writing to voice my strong support for your curriculum. It has already reached a great number of students and the teachers have testified to the fact that it has been highly successful.

The character education students receive is very much in need and the fact that it is embedded in a sophisticated writing curriculum makes it easy for the teachers to use. The affective education this curriculum cultivates often reinforces what is being taught in the home, and for some, offers essential instruction not experienced in the home.

I believe this project can make a difference in our students and our society.

Frank R. Elliot Ed. D.
Superintendent of Schools
Ross Valley School District

In my work at the Joseph Campbell Foundation, I have reviewed many mythological education programs, and while each has been well-intended, most have been limited by their focus on either "the hero's journey" (as a paradigm for personal growth) or on the development of a "personal mythology", and almost all have been directed at adults or "older" students.

Big Philosophy for Little Kids, however, stands in marked contrast to these other programs. This unique writing curriculum is distinctive in its use of mythological narratives as the contextual base for the development of character. I whole-heartedly recommend it to all educators seeking a particularly meaningful program for younger students. Neither you nor they will be disappointed.

Robert Walter, President
Joseph Campbell Foundation

Never before has the bell rung so clearly for character development curriculum in elementary school education. For educators, parents, and children alike, this curriculum offers touching and unique activities that promise to both develop character and shape the culture in which we live. This is the kind of education that could benefit every school district in America.

Michael Murphy, Esalen Founder; Author of
Golf in the Kingdom and *The Future of the Body*

Your project to recover the legacy of ancient understanding and wisdom for students today is not just a noble undertaking but an essential one. That legacy lies at the foundation of our cultural tradition; its structures and principles still inform the depth of our collective psyche. Our age urgently needs to reconnect with this treasure, and there is no more important place to begin that task than with the education of the young. I am genuinely impressed by the insight, creativity, and gentleness with which you have engaged that effort.

Richard Tarnas, Phd.
Professor of Philosophy & Psychology,
California Institute of Integral Studies
Author, *The Passion of the Western Mind*

Parents

I express my whole-hearted support for the Royal Games Program. Both of my children have participated in sessions. My daughter participated as a fourth grader. My son received training as a second grader. I am a second grade teacher at another school.

If you are a parent, you are probably aware of how little children are willing to talk at home about school. Both of my children would share at the dinner table the game they played that day. They shared it in a thoughtful way expressing feelings as well as retelling the event. This illustrates to me the impact these Games had on my children. My seven year old son learned a vocabulary to categorize human behavior. For example he would say, 'He is being greedy like King Midas.' We vacationed in Montana and visited the Battle of Bighorn site. We were able to convey a picture of Custer to the children by saying he was like Narcissus. My nine year old daughter also gained vocabulary, but more importantly started to define her value system. She saw consistency, concentration, compassion and self-knowledge as valuable traits. She personally was dealing with some fears; nightmares were difficult for her. By using the Royal Breaths she was able to control the panic she was feeling. It has been a tool she has used many times.

I have given only a few illustrations of how the Royal Games have effected my children. There are many more. The wisdom they gained by these activities and discussions will stay with them for a lifetime.

Amy Anderson, Mother & 1st Grade Teacher

Teachers

It is now obvious that great ideas inspire great writing.

Dan Alderson, AP English teacher, Sonoma Valley HS, CA

...[This curriculum]empowered me as a teacher and I am certain they have empowered my students — and even those who know my students. It has become an integral part of my teaching. I fully expect to use and develop it for my whole life.

Susan Phaneuf
Sanchez Elementary School, San Francisco, CA

...I sincerely believe that there will be an enduring influence on the children from having participated in the Royal Games. I already have witnessed this strong influence on their behavior in the areas of improved attention skills; greater empathy for others; and improved ability to deal with peer relationships.

Joan Taylor
Brookside Elementary, San Anselmo, CA

Letters and Writing Examples from the Kids

About a week ago I said to my sister, "I bet you I can climb higher than you can on the tree." So she said, "Let's see."

So we went outside and I thought it would be easy for me since she is only six. So I started to climb up as fast as I could go so it would be over with, but when I was not high up, I slipped and fell, but I did not hurt myself a lot. But when my sister tried she focused and almost got to the top and beat me.

Cause I was being Icarus and she was being Daedalus.

Martin, San Anselmo, CA (age 9)

A lifelong lesson that I will always remember is to be focused and concentrate to get something done well.

James, San Francisco, CA (age 11)

You have taught me so much I don't know how to repay you. I will always remember the royal breaths because I always use them. I will remember deep happiness. I will remember high happiness and how it has less meaning. I will always remember to be like Daedalus and focused and not to be like Icarus and impulsive. But most importantly I will not be like Narcissus. I will care and have empathy for others. You are great for teaching me this.

Terry, Fairfax, CA (age 10)

Scope and Sequence

Unit One: Attention!
Teaching Our Children to Focus, Persist, and Rest

Unit Two: Tell Me a Story
Children Practice Self-Expression While Exercising the Features of Story-Telling

---

Unit Three: Brief and Long-Lasting Happiness
Dynamic Writing on Wisdom

Unit Four: Self-Knowledge
Children Compose Simple Self-Understanding

Unit Five: Response-Ability
The Responsive Paragraph; Breath and Feeling

Unit Six: The Developmental Rainbow
Writing Full Essays On Growing Up, Exercising Parallelism and Personalizations

---

Unit Seven: Service Heroes
Integrating Research, Art, Poetry, and Taking Character

Appendices

"If you are planning for a year, sow rice;

if you are planning for a decade, plant trees;

if you are planning for a lifetime, educate people."

- Chinese proverb

For the next epoch

Teacher Introduction and Full Overview

Big Philosophy for Little Kids teaches writing and language arts skills while academically considering traditional and universal wisdoms in "affective" areas. *Affective education* includes emotional fluency and expression, character education, social intelligence and basic moral clarity. **This multi-cultural, standards-based curriculum had been designed to raise test scores as it provides teachers with a detailed and exciting writing program. Simple enough for English-learners while abundantly sophisticated, this curriculum strengthens the children both academically and affectively.** *Big Philosophy for Little Kids* is infused with writing, reading, and comprehension skills, vocabulary development, word analysis, and a wide range of affective issues and social studies. (**USA Common Core Standards** are indicated at the fifth grade level and easily adapted to grades 2-7+.) It has been used in the public and private sectors for over 20 years in a variety of socio-economic cultures. Children everywhere love this.

Big Philosophy for Little Kids exercises the features of "long-term" writing projects combined with meaningful affective education, rather than teaching them in isolation. *Big Philosophy for Little Kids* easily integrates other writing programs into it, especially those that teach writing traits and modes. Teachers may continue to use their favorite writing techniques with the themes herein and find your District's writing prompts addressed. To make the lessons clear, examples from my inner city students are evident.

This curriculum is an "integral" program not only because it integrates multiple subject areas, but because it addresses the human being in personal and social domains, in behaviorial as well as feeling dimensions. For a brief introduction to Integral Theory and and the complex issues surrounding affective education, please see the Appendix.

Rather than having a separate program on character strengths and emotional fluency, these issues are naturally integrated into a language arts curriculum that empowers the writing activities with personal meaning. *Seeing how patterns of experience are intertwined with feelings and behavior is the essence of affective responsibility.* This feeling-understanding ("behind" behavior) empowers our relational capacities and self-understanding. Feeling is indeed the ground of respect. The deep meaning suggested by wise tales empowers self-authentication and relational feelings — making writing most real. Or in the simpler words of my colleague, Dan Alderson, "Great ideas empower great writing." In using this curriculum, you will not only teach the children to write with power, you will empower them (and their world).

*****

Unit One begins with the inspirational story of Wilma Rudolph, an amazing woman, full of spirit and wisdom, whose tale is useful to anyone learning concentration and persistence. The wisdom and demonstration of "poor," "crippled", "colored" Wilma is an easy icon for children to understand. Against all odds, she ascended into the Games of Olympia and utter glory. Through her heroics and advice, children are inspired and challenged to cultivate a life with a greater focus— joined with "learning how to fail". This story and easy writing assignment is integrated into the home life in a manner that makes the caregiver a kind of hero (they interview their parents/caregivers on an event or period in their lives that was extremely difficult and the children write that story for the teacher). Another feature of attention specifically clarified is the exercise of restraint. Students learn to exercise temperance in the fun game "Start-Stop'. Enhancing the awareness of attention is a "Studenthood Report Card", whereby the students grade themselves (with their parents) on the qualities of attention they exhibit at home and school. (They naturally apply this clarification to their own lives and schoolwork, no preaching is needed.) This introduction to the course (like most units), contains meaningful activities, self-involvement, and challenges. Here, we discern several attributes of developing attention.

With the story of Wilma Rudolph, we also begin "Comprehension Creation", whereby the students make up their own test (to exchange or self-apply) and create their own "focus questions" for the story itself. "Comprehension Creation" puts the ownership of comprehension onto the student -- it does not come from without, but from authentic thinking. This activity is repeated throughout this curriculum so that authentic comprehension is an established skill.

Unit Two is about emotional expressions in the art of writing. It begins in *My Fun Story*, or more fully, *From Across the Parking Lot and Up the Elevator to My Fun Story*. Here, the children expressively make their own simple, illustrated book/story, learning the basic parts of story-telling and the writing process along the way. Using the foundations of "telling" and drawing, I have found that my weakest students shine here, giving them a beginning-of-the-year confidence and "buy in" to the tasks involved in writing. "My Fun Story" is a student-directed story of their own expression, about anything they want. The teacher initially teaches Main Idea ad Setting with the Writing Process — and <u>then</u> Character and Plot. Even English learners illustrate, write, and produce their own small book.

Unit Two also contains several lessons for language development. A few, easy autobiographical exercises prepares the students for a variety of assessments — giving the students an exercise in poetic, emotional, and logical self-expression. With an appreciation of personal history and their story-creation fresh in their experience, we quickly engage the rich story of *The Legend of English* — where we develop comprehension strategies, word recognition, vocabulary development, and unearth the etymological strands of the English language. With their own personal timeline in their recent memory, children engage a chronicle that starts with the Roman founding of London ~ 44BCE, and, with this linguistic emphasis on the history of English, they are introduced to a timeline that covers the broad phases of Western history over the last 2000+ years.

The *Legend of English* serves two functions: 1) to illustrate the strands, sources, and development of English within Western history, and 2) to locate key incidents and discoveries in the developments of social studies and science within the timeline. This quick lesson on word appreciation provides a calendared context for the rest of the year, illuminating a variety of historical occasions, across many subject areas.

Naturally, the children come to quickly understand the fall of the Roman Empire, the Dark Ages, the Renaissance, along with seeing the creation of Old, Middle, and Modern English. I also use the History Channel's "The Dark Ages" and pause at select, vibrant scenes and have the children practice "Show, Not Tell" quickwrites.

With the legend of English comprehended, students are introduced to the chart *The Body of English* (a la` DaVinci) whereby the trunk is labeled *Germanic*, the throat and arms are labeled *French*, the head labeled *Greek*, and the legs labeled *Latin*—accounting for 97% of the most common words in the English language—visually addressing educational requirements for the study of etymology. More importantly, this imagery impresses the children with a somatic as well as visual experience of the "body" that is English. As a large poster, it is a great "word wall".

The Body of English is followed by another "Comprehension Creation", where students make their own questions for a test on *The Legend of English* for their parents, using question stems lifted from the 2010 State of California Assessment and Reporting (STAR) tests. I call these academically imbedded question stems, "Questions from STARs." [STAR was replaced by the California Assessment of Student Performance and Progress CAASPP.] Nevertheless, these linguistic forms familiarize students, particularly English learners, with question structures in academic English and interrogatory orders of understanding. The questions the students generate are then pooled (according to the art of the teacher) for a class test. This pre-post-create (Listen-See-Do) Comprehension strategy is designed to make comprehension scores rise by doing it right. The school looks good, you look good, the parents are engaged, and the students show more of their greatness in a way they are happy to embrace.

Unit Three plays upon the dynamic of brief and long-lasting happiness. Was King Midas truly happy when he had endless gold? Was he deeply happy when his beloved daughter changed back from gold to hug him? Thus, the children begin a full essay (in my District, at the early part of 5th grade, this is 1-2 pages), using Contrast-Compare strategies and two-point paragraph construction to address and appreciate both kinds of happiness. This distinction between the happiness of things and the happiness at your feeling core forms a central tenet in virtually every system of human thought. This is values education at its most universal core. You'll see wisdom coming from the mouths of children.

Unit Four exercises the self-knowledge and sobriety that is necessary for harmonious living. Children are guided into the natural observance and confession of over-much self-orientation, first through the myth of Narcissus. A natural humility is inherited when we acknowledge this universality. And humility is not thinking less of yourself, as CS Lewis pointed out, but thinking of your self less. Children learn to discern harmonious and healthy self-empowerment from overly selfish self-concern.

Self-knowledge is furthered by the stories the children make up about the juxtaposed twins, *Damonia* and *Destiny*. Using these images, we highlight the universal observation of ways that you can be responsible for how you are feeling, and how you are feeling not only affects how you see things, but the kinds of experiences your feelings invoke. Balancing both sides of the brain, students consider wise choices as they again exercise a variety of writing traits, again exercising setting, character, plot, descriptive language, and figures of speech, while keeping in mind point of view, audience, and message.

Unit Five considers a world of wisdom and response-ability. *R-E-S-P-O-N-D* is an activity that requires students to respond to salient and famous quotes from around the world in several different ways — forming the basis for developing a responsive essay. The chosen quotes are grouped for use according to the theme being addressed in the lesson. (English Learners make translations of the quotes as an activity.) After the *R-E-S-P-O-N-D* activity is established, students learn and exercise five kinds of concluding sentences (and then choose the best one). An essay finalizes the lesson and brings all the pieces together in a focused singularity.

Unit Five also teaches the ways and advantages of using your breath. Drawing upon wisdom traditions from India to Hellas to Africa, the use of the breath is investigated, both by story and by self-authenticating experience.

Unit Six climaxes in a responsive essay (3-6 pages in length) that exercises the writing techniques of parallelism and personalization. The children respond to the developmental nuances of childhood as they respond to each piece of the essay "What is it to really grow up?" Herein, students learn extensive note-taking as well as exercise personalization and writing in parallels.

Unit Seven is the finale as students investigate and make a report/presentation on a "Service Hero or Heroine". Examples: Martin Luther King, Jr., Aung Sung Suu Kyi, John Muir, Mahatma Ghandi, Helen Keller, Caesar Chavez, Kong Qiu, and Greta Thunberg, so on... Here students take character, acting as their hero, and they also contemplate how they would like to help.

Big Philosophy for Little Kids carries an inspiring scope and long-term sequence in practical detail for teachers in the middle grades. The tools herein can be used in part or in whole. The details of this curriculum are reverse-engineered to satisfy the simple needs of English Language Learners in the fifth grade, even while providing instruction and enrichment for advanced students in higher grades. Adjust according to your art and in sensitivity to the students before you each new day.

The Art of Teaching

There is an art whereby a teacher elicits learning, elicits participation, elicits creativity and growth. It is the art of openness, challenge, and invitation. In developing this art, the teacher sees through skin color and gender, sees through the façade of social faces, and sees through every act of need and fear. The teacher sees clearly the spark or light that is at the core of each and every one, sees how to invite that livingness into openness and trust, sees how to tend that spark into a fire and that vibrancy into genius.

When the teacher matures in this dual-sensitivity of graciousness and growing demand, she or he becomes a kind of priest or priestess, artfully attending the sacred fires who are their students. To invite children into the joy of continual growth, one must be involved in a practice of continual growth. Inspirational teaching is spiritual, attending to the spirit of each student. To lead children out of inability and reactivity to response-ability is not openness only, but openness joined with spirited challenge and gracious appreciation.

A great teacher's "spiritual x-ray vision" sees clearly a unique moment in the interaction with children: the first split second when your eyes meet theirs. For if you look through your social face and theirs, you can always see the question that riddles the flesh and complicates every soul: "Are you going to hurt me?" Capturing that initiation, the great teacher is prepared. Deep in her or his heart, he or she is already chanting, "I see you, I'll care for you". In an instant, the student sees the teacher as a friend and the teacher's caring eyes plant a seed of hope in their heart. The first split second when your eyes meet theirs is a great opportunity, and only care and vigilance are required to catch it.

The art of teaching is to tender that place in every child that nobly responds to the call to grow.

Unit I: Attention!

Teaching Children to Focus, Persist, and Rest

The Secret: The Story of Wilma Rudolph

The Attention Muscle
One Pointedness, One Minute
The Mountain of Attention
Self-Challenges
Interviewing Caregiver and Writing
Restraint: "Start-Stop"
Studenthood Report Card

Common Core Standards Addressed:
Reading
Lit. 1, 2, 4, 9
Reading Foundational Skills 4a, 9a

Writing
Narratives 3a, b, d; 4, 5, 9a, 10

Speaking and Listening
4b Recitation

The Task of Concentration & The Wisdom of Failure

Big Philosophy for Little Kids begins with lessons on attention. The task of improving attention anchors the lessons as well as the student. This strengthening attention provides a firm foundation for the rest of life (especially schoolwork!) and grounds the child in self-generated improvement.

When attention itself becomes a distinct subject, students naturally participate in their own growth. While studying and teaching the challenge of attention, a primary focus is perseverance, but everyone tends to forget that persistence is only one half of the reality of accomplishment. To emphasize persistence alone belittles the difficulty of the task and weakens one's resolve. A proper relationship to frustration and failure is also required — and is to be emphasized along with improving attention.

To embrace both these positive and "negative" aspects of attention stabilizes one's growth in a full-rounded reality. Give encouragement and guidance in concentrating, persistence, and excellence, but also share extensively about the difficulty of losing and letting go of the embarrassment of falling and failing. Let us not rob our children of the night.

To actively focus and to persist are fundamental requirements in every human undertaking. We must explicitly teach and challenge our children to focus and persist. But to persist with growing strength, we must forgive ourselves of our failures—and come to rest—before or as we try again. Thus it is said, "The best athletes have the shortest memory." Otherwise we are trapped in the wasteful moods of reaction. By acceptance and rest, we are able to respond (response-ability) in the moment, rather than re-acting to a past event. Therefore, in addition to persistence, the other great component of the theme of attention is rest. To increase the capacity of attention, we must not only exercise our focus, not only persevere in that focus, we must also learn to rest. This stillness, acceptance, or rest is the receptive component of attention—and, let your children know, very difficult.

Trying, persistence, falling short, and acceptance. Again and again and again. Strenthening the attention muscle. Slowly and surely.

Let us invite our children into a great process; let them know that this challenge of attention is a lifetime challenge, a muscle that they will forever attend to, not something they are going to get right or wrong. Because children tend to see in black-and-white, explicitly let them know it is a process; there is no failure or unending winning, only growing slowly or urgently.

The real-life stories of Wilma Rudolph, (see also the companion volume *Core Stories* with Glenn Cunningham, and The Mighty Atom) not only illustrate the exercise of attention, they also describe the process of a full recovery. Everyone, at some time, has a recovery in front of them.

In other stories you engage with your child or your class, always highlight the characters' relation to frustration and failure. Tell the story of when Michael Jordon got cut from the basketball team in high school. Or Nelson Mandela, Mahatma Ghandi, Aung San Suu Kyi, Martin Luther King Jr. in prison, or when addressing younger children, *The Little Engine That Could*, etc. Consistently emphasize the theme of frustration and temporary failure, how it makes you feel, how failure makes you want to quit; and then emphasize and demonstrate the proper relation to frustration and failure.

Always lead your children into a process of growth, not only good or only bad. A proper relation to failure makes persistence distinct and strong. This inclusion of failure and frustration sets the stage for growing attention and the rewards of persistence.

Do not preach, but guide and praise, tell them stories, and reveal your own process. This interplay of failure, patience, attention, persistence, acceptance, and healing can be most easily clarified by hearing the story of another.

*****

One of the secrets of these lessons is that *attention itself* is made into a *unique* subject. The direct exercise of attention is made into a specific challenge as the students are called to build their "attention muscle".

In preparation to the writing assignment, and to imbue this lesson with meaning, your students hear the story of Wilma Rudolph and then engage in role play about what it is like to concentrate, fail, persist, and succeed. The students learn to recognize their own collapse around failure, how to recognize, accept, and let go of bad feelings, and also to recognize the intelligence of persistence through the failures they encounter.

Procedure:

- Go over the Vocabulary Preparation -- as needed for your students. In my inner-city classes, this could require a large block of time. (Great investment.) As they read the story, identification of these words is invited.
- Read and/or guide your students in reading or listening to the story of Wilma Rudolf -- and when you come to the part in the story where Wilma walked again for the first time without falling, pause the story and initiate a demonstration.

1. **Tell them** they will pretend to be Wilma and soon slowly stand, holding onto their desk, *as if it were* the first time.

2. Before the demonstration/act, **ask** the children to imagine what it would be like. Would the legs shake or be steady? How would they 'hold on'? What would their balance be like?

3. When you get to the part in the story where Wilma walks for the first time in her church, **invite** all your children to stand and take a few steps <u>without falling</u> like Wilma did. After this participatory scene from Wilma's childhood, lead your children to contemplate the actions and feelings of young Wilma. Generate a list of emotions encountered in persistence.

4. Have students **share examples** of situations when they experienced these feelings and when they persisted. Read the rest of the story.

*****

Note: This foundational lesson is one of the most developed in the curriculum and requires a series of lessons. The preparation for the writing assignment is extensive and nuanced. Fret not, the rewards of this beginning lesson will be harvested all year long.

Note: The anchor story and all others (as well as Parent Guides) are also in the student reader: *Core Stories.*

Note: The vocabulary pages for every story and most charts are available for download at www.frankmarrero.com. Feel free to massage and alter these lessons, charts, and assignments according to your needs and art.

Adapt this story to your own students, the format and Common Core Standards given here are decidedly fifth-grade, but I have used versions successfully in grades 2 through 8.

Note: All stories (and student-directed text) herein are in a larger type for ease of reproduction for classroom use.

Vocabulary Preparation for "Against All Odds: Wilma Rudolph"

Vocabulary words in every unit were selected by my 5th grade English Language Learners. As such, they provide a comprehensive guide to vocabulary needs, so adjust accordingly. Vocabulary preparation is **foundational** to understanding text. I give out these words one page at a time and have the students discuss possible meanings and then share their knowledge: "Give one, get one," as Sharroky Hollie says. Then we concur as a group, page by page. I find it most useful for the children to have/create a vocabulary-building manual and put these words in it. Fill in as you go and make vocabulary building as active and interactive as possible! Group activities and classroom challenges (*Jeapordy!*-like games) can enliven this task. At the end of one unit, I challenged my students to make up their own interesting way to review our new vocabulary words. They made a fashion show and game using reviewed words upon paper as material for group creations.

Note: The following vocabulary list is **long** and may require significant preparation.

Against All Odds: Wilma Rudolph

pneumonia _____

remedy _____

fragile _____

defy _____

sorrow _____

paralyzed _____

persistence _____

submitting _____

electrified _____

collapsing _____

autobiography _____

obsessed _____

devastated _____

infirmary _____

necessity _____

rejuvenating _____

rejected _____

effect _____

dedicated _____

accomplishment _____

spectacular _____

determination _____

Olympics _____

competitor _____

imprisonment _____

physical _____

affection _____

microphone _____

photographer _____

reality _____

barrier _____

motorcade _____

accepted _____

terrified _____

peer _____

aisle _____

effort _____

improvement _____

courage _____

vowed _____

strengthened _____

delirious _____

banquet _____

escorted _____

trounced _____

spirit _____

nod _____

requests _____

immense _____

greeted _____

disabled _____

droves (not past-tense of "drives")_____

recruited _____

disqualified _____

integrated _____

inspiring _____

mayor _____

resolve _____

gender _____

score (the kind that is a special number!)_____

undaunted _____

rescued _____

baton _____

bobbled _____

triumphed _____

banner _____

Against All Odds: Wilma Rudolph

The story of Wilma Rudolph is an inspiring story about an African American woman overcoming severe physical handicaps, emotional difficulties, and social barriers.

Wilma Rudolph was born in the small country town of Clarksville, just outside of Nashville, Tennessee, in 1940. She was the 20th of 22 children, and due to a fall by her mother, was born at home, two months premature, tiny and weak. Medical care was out of the question for her poor family, and was mainly available to educated whites. The closest hospital for blacks was 40 miles away in Nashville. Wilma Rudolph was not expected to live.

Wilma's mother took care of her anyway, gave Wilma all her love and affection. But Wilma was so tiny and fragile she got every cold and sickness that came through town. Her mother gave her home remedies and put her under piles of blankets to sweat out the bad stuff. That worked on the measles, mumps and chicken pox; she lived through all of those—even when other kids around her died. At age four, she came down with double pneumonia and then scarlet fever. Once again, she should have died. Then the worst thing of all happened, she got the awful crippling disease: polio.

Polio bent and paralyzed her legs and the doctors told her that she would never walk again. (Imagine that you are a tiny kid who has been sick almost all of your life, and the doctors tell you that you will never walk again.) Wilma was crushed with sorrow and despair. But her mother had another notion—that they would defy the odds. Wilma later recalled, "The doctors told me I would never walk, but my mother told me I would, so I believed in my mother."

Wilma's mother carried her twice a week to Meharry Medical College 40 miles away in Nashville. Wilma recalled, "Always a greyhound bus, always the same route, and always the people who were black sat in the back." Once at the hospital, they massaged and moved her legs. She tried to help too, even though the sessions were very painful. Soon her mother learned how to do everything and gave her physical therapy at home. While other kids her age started school, Wilma was left at home, her useless leg strapped into a heavy metal brace. In some ways this was her hardest battle; being alone, not being able to play with any of her friends. Wilma wrote in her autobiography, "Being left behind had a terrible effect. I was so lonely, and I felt rejected. I would close my eyes, and just drift off into a sinking feeling, going down, down, down. I cried a lot."

During this time Clarksville's only African American doctor would come and visit her, free of charge. Dr. Coleman was a bridge over troubled waters for her at this time. Wilma recalled, "He would come by the house every so often to check up on me; I remember him well, he was such a beautiful man. He was so kind and nice, and never pressured the poor black people for money . . . He would say, 'Wilma, everything is gonna turn out all right. You just fight this thing, you understand?'"

At night Wilma's mom would come home after a long day at work, and after she cooked dinner for her family of two dozen, she would devote herself to serving Wilma, even though she was as tired as tired can be. She would massage and move Wilma's legs and tell her it was gonna be fine someday. Wilma's therapy hurt a lot, but the hurt was kinda good; at least there was some life in her legs. But Wilma still felt like a sick little kid and still seemed to get every flu or cold that came along. She was almost always sick. One day however, when she was starting to come down with a sore throat, she got mad. Instead of collapsing and submitting to another infirmary, she screamed to herself, "Life cannot be about being sick all the time. Enough! No more taking everything that comes along, no more drifting off, no more wondering. Enough is enough!"

And what do you think began to happen? Wilma Rudolph began to fight, she would stand up to her sorrow, stand up to feeling sorry for herself, fight through the pain in her legs, try harder even if it hurt, and she began to develop her inner spirit, build her attention, and strengthen her focus.

But she got only a little better. She tried and tried with all her might, day after day, week after week, month after month—with no progress. She tried with all her attention, but every day she failed. Another day's hope had become the daily failure. Even still, she learned to accept her reality and her necessity, and so rested fully at day's end, because she gave her best.

Sometimes she wanted to quit, but didn't. Other times she did quit, but later began again. For years she kept up her courage and persistence, even though there was little improvement.

When she finally did get to go to school on braces and crutches she was not brave or even excited, but frightened. "I had been alone so much of my life that I was terrified of my own peer group. I knew I was poor, moneywise that is, and I knew my clothes were made by my mother and not bought in some fancy store."

Wilma wanted more than anything in the world to be accepted by her classmates. But they made fun of her braces and crutches and she was crushed again. She had been a failure everyday, dreaming of the day she would get to go to school. Now at school she felt like a failure again. She wanted to do something that none of her classmates would do so that she would be great and then her classmates would have to like her.

She worked extra hard at getting her legs stronger. For months there was no improvement, but Wilma did not give up. After another year, only the slightest improvement and her extra effort did not even seem to be helping. She still walked with crutches and a leg brace. But she didn't give up. Another whole year went by and again the most frustrating tiny improvement, but it was improvement. Wilma didn't give up. Another year went by and finally she could stand without her leg brace and take a step or two. But she would fall every time and it always hurt. Even then she wouldn't give up.

Finally, just before her tenth birthday, came the day she had been waiting for. She dressed in her Sunday best clothes and went to church. She waited until everybody else went in and sat down. When she got to the front door, she took off her braces and walked all the way down the aisle. Every eye was on her, everyone was so proud of her, every heart wished her the best.

Wilma was so happy she felt like she had exploded. She could feel the spirit of happiness rejuvenating her poor little body. Even her fragile and sickly legs could be transformed. Everyday she practiced walking without her brace, like a baby learning to walk. And slowly, like a baby, it took her two more years before her next goal was reached: she could walk all day without falling and she took off her brace forever. She sent it back to the hospital with a note of thanks and suggested that another kid could now use it.

Wilma Rudolph had fulfilled her dream of proving her mother right and the doctors wrong. But more importantly she had learned how to persist through failure and frustration. Her attention was great, her focus sharp, and now, after eight years of constant struggle and metal imprisonment, she was healthy and happy. Now she had the right stuff to set her spirit to the extra-ordinary.

Entering the seventh grade, Wilma took up basketball and tried out for the team. Even though she was the weakest kid, she had one advantage: when Coach Gray asked the kids for long and hard practices, Wilma could outlast everyone else. Not because she was the strongest, but only because she was the most determined. She made the team.

Wilma continued to work harder than her teammates, and even practiced for hours after the team practice had finished, but did not get to play in real games except for the last couple of minutes if her team was far ahead or far behind. Wilma wanted to be a starter.

And the next year was the same, Wilma warmed the bench. But instead of quitting, she practiced harder than ever. Her persistence earned her the nickname 'Skeeter', slang for mosquito. Even still she only warmed the bench. "I used to sit there on the bench and dream about someday becoming a star for the team, but the coach didn't seem to know I was alive."

Finally, after two long frustrating years, she confronted Coach Gray: she wanted a spot on the starting team. The coach listened but said nothing. But when game time came Wilma got the nod and her spirit electrified the whole team. They played with such spirit they trounced the other team.

News of Wilma's play spread through the town. People came in droves to see the little girl who had only recently shed her braces play in competition. And Wilma was not just a popular starter, she quickly became a star, racking up points, and inspiring her whole team.

Wilma Rudolph's spirit took their team to the state championships, where they had to first play another strong team. Undaunted, Wilma tossed in 26 points to lead her team to another triumph. The next team was a weak team and Wilma and her crew thought they would beat them easily. They dreamed they were going to win the whole thing and go on to be the Cinderellas of basketball. They did not bring their usual focus and attention to the game and the weaker team beat them.

Wilma was devastated. They had not been defeated by hardship, but by themselves. Wilma vowed that she would focus not only when it was hard, but also when it looked like it was easy too. Thinking too much of herself had brought defeat upon her. Obsessed with losing or winning consumes your attention and then you don't have enough left over for actually focusing! Wilma vowed to strengthen her attention even more, beyond winning or losing. Her only concern would be her attention, with giving fully, giving when she wanted to let up, giving more and more; competing only with herself, on focusing now, on trying harder or trying again—winning or not. Her resolve let her also rest fully and deeply when she was not giving her attention. She vowed not be depressed by losing nor be big-headed by winning, but to stay focused only on doing her best, resting in dedication.

Continuing to strengthen her attention muscle beyond losing and winning, Wilma had learned a great secret.

"Winning is great, sure, but if you are going to do something in life, *the secret is learning how to lose.* Nobody goes undefeated all the time. If you can pick yourself up after a defeat, and go on to win again, you can be a champion."

Wilma was recruited by a college track coach named Ed Temple to take up running. She brought the same attention and dedication to running that she had to basketball. The little disabled girl had grown into a runner!

Wilma learned the hard way (that is by losing!), the skills of her new sport. And when she had learned those skills from Coach Temple, she took off like a bullet.

Within a year she was the youngest person on the US Olympic team! Only four years earlier she was wearing braces! Now the little girl from the country town of Clarksville, Tennessee travelled to the other side of the world to compete for the

United States in the 1956 Australian Olympics. She was sixteen, six foot tall, and only weighed 90 pounds. But, for the first time in her life, Wilma Rudolph felt like no one cared if the color of her skin was dark. She was just another competitor, another spirited champion amongst spirited champions. Spirit cares not for the color or size or gender, but only for trying and shining and caring.

Wilma did not make any of the cuts she needed to compete in the championship races in Australia, but her team did make the relay race. She felt failure again, but now it only strengthened her resolve. Wilma's performance made the difference in the relay race, and they captured a bronze medal. She was proud and amazed and very happy.

When her parents greeted her at the airport in Nashville, everything was complete. Now Wilma had a new determination. She would be back in the next Olympics.

In 1960, four years later, Wilma made the Olympic team again and went to Rome to go for the gold. In her first two events, she not only took the golds, she also set new world records.

In her final race, she was the last leg of the relay, and by the time the baton came to her, her team was behind. Worst still, she almost bobbled the baton which would have disqualified her. But Wilma caught her attention just in time and took off like lightning, running faster than any woman had ever, ever run before. At the end, she put on a spectacular burst of speed and inched ahead of her competitors. The crowds went crazy for her.

"The feeling of accomplishment welled up inside me . . . three Olympic gold medals. I knew that was something nobody could ever take away from me, ever. After the playing of the 'Star-Spangled Banner,' I was mobbed. People were jumping all over me, pushing microphones into my face, pounding my back. I had to be rescued by the American officials."

Now Wilma Rudolph was a world hero; the little disabled girl had shown them! She had proven to everyone how spirit and determination had transformed dead flesh into light. Requests poured in for her company. Pope John XXIII received her and then Wilma and her team traveled to visit the leaders of Europe. When they returned to New York, Wilma was mobbed. One fan even tore her shoes off of her feet; the entire country was delirious with her accomplishment.

When she finally got back to Nashville, another immense crowd welcomed her. "Everybody was there—mayors of cities, the state governor, judges, tv stations, marching bands, scores of reporters and photographers." A police motorcade escorted her to Clarksville for her victory party. Thousands of people lined the highway waving at her. Banners hung across the streets and when she arrived in Clarksville, the entire town, black and white, turned out to greet her. And all because Wilma had insisted it be so. "It was actually the first integrated event in the history of the town. So was the banquet they gave for me that night; it was the first time in Clarksville's history that blacks and whites had gathered under the same roof for the same event."

*****

The spirit of giving creates a great celebration, and sees through all color and false limits to a kinder and stronger light.

Wilma died suddenly of brain cancer in 1994, but her spirit will always shine.

After the story is comprehended, appreciated, and discussed, introduce the following role play activity:

The Attention Muscle

Teacher Prompt:

"When you focus, is it like this (dramatically tense your bicep as an archetype of work and strength) or like this (relax arm)?

(DISCUSSION)

"Yes, attention is like a muscle. (tense arm again). How do you make a muscle get stronger?

(DISCUSSION)

"Does it get stronger all at once or a little bit over a long time?"

(DISCUSSION)

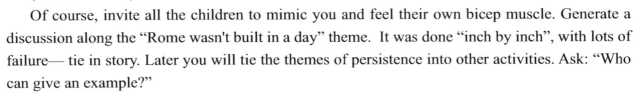

Of course, invite all the children to mimic you and feel their own bicep muscle. Generate a discussion along the "Rome wasn't built in a day" theme. It was done "inch by inch", with lots of failure— tie in story. Later you will tie the themes of persistence into other activities. Ask: "Who can give an example?"

POINT OUT: At-tention is just like a-tension; tensing the attention muscle makes it stronger and stronger, just like any other muscle. All the while, show a bodily expression of strength (e.g. bulging bicep) and encourage the children to do likewise. Getting stronger is about exercising attention; attention grows like any muscle. It just takes some exercise.

Quick Activity: "One Pointedness, One Minute"
(Kinesthetic reinforcement)

Draw a single dot on the whiteboard and invite a child to take a marker and draw a circle around it. Then tell that child to hand the marker to another child. Repeat this until you have something like a series of concentric circles (hopefully). I use the teachable moment of pointing out the relationship of "concentric" and "concentrate"!

Teacher Prompt/Demonstration:

"OK, now that we have created a 'bulls-eye' series of concentric circles, let me tell you a secret about attention. If you can learn to focus on one point, you can learn to do most anything because attention is used in everything. Part of this secret is to concentrate your eyes. Like this:" (Demonstrate)

At this point, invite everyone to concentrate on the point at the center of the class-created bulls-eye on the board <u>while standing on one foot</u> (or not) for sixty seconds. (Adapt these instructions to your class, of course.)

Classroom Management Tip: *Pre-address* your kids tendencies to silliness, laughter, and using this theatre as a personal stage. Let them know that inattention is just weakness in this exercise -- and give them clear avenues to calmly rejoin the activity. Remind them that learning to build strong attention is difficult.

After one minute, ask if they would like to try it for longer. Use the following activity as a way to test and expand this theme of concentrated attention:

"One Pointedness, One Minute"

"Now, let's look at the center of the clock (or the bulls-eye you have collectively made) and try and focus on it for one full minute. Don't look at anything else other than the one tiny dot.

"If you begin to fall, go ahead and stand on both feet for a big, full breath, letting go of any bad feelings about falling and failing. Just stay focused. Become completely still again, then start holding your attention on a single point and standing on one foot again. Change feet if you get tired, just hold on to the still point with your eyes. Does everybody understand? OK, on your mark, get set, let's start. *"*

After your initial trial, add the following "distraction challenge".

"OK, that was good. But now I will try and distract you, I will try to make you look away, but your job is to be absolutely still, not wiggling or giggling, but completely focused."

"Distraction Challenge"

As the kids become focused, attempt to distract them in humorous ways; make faces, roar, wave your hands, etc. Once they are successful with this level of focus, tell them you are going to make it really hard for them and ceremoniously pull out a large feather (with a semi-wicked look on your face)! Now have them focus again, but this time go around and lightly tickle their ears. They love this dramatization.

Joan Owen, a fourth grade teacher in San Anselmo, California, gives the children an object to focus on as she uses a feather and tries to get them to laugh and lose their focus.

Praise those that keep focused and encourage the others who laugh or fall to keep trying. Reaffirm the importance on stillness and quiet as part of the challenge. When children "fall" or hop madly or otherwise attract attention, gently remind them to exercise their attention muscle and come to stillness again.

Classroom Management Tips

• Remind your children (as often as your art allows), that they are learning to *give* attention not *get* attention.

• My students collectively earn points for good, attentive time that they can cash in for free minutes for skits or dance on Friday afternoons.

*****

Image to keep in mind and reinforce: The Mountain of Attention

After the "One Pointedness" activities, introduce the image of *A Mountain of Attention*.

Teacher prompts to invite discussion/participation:

• "Imagine taking a spoonful of dirt and pouring it in some place, and doing it again and again until you have a mound. Now imagine every time you do something that really takes your attention you add a spoonful to your mound. How large a mound can you build? By the time you have grown up, hopefully you will have built a mountain of attention!"

• "Would you like to have a mountain of attention? Do you realize how hard that will be? Imagine building a whole mountain a spoonful at a time!"

• "But if you build a mountain of attention, you will have a key to a thousand doors. Well, we are all paying attention everyday and building our mountain, aren't we? Can you say, 'I am a mound builder'?"

•"Building a mound is hard, for sure, and mountain of attention is even harder. Sometimes you have to persist in things like doing the dishes, cleaning your room, doing your homework or actually climbing a really big hill or running fast, or playing a musical instrument. What are some other examples when attention is really hard?"

Comprehension *Creation*
(Common Core Standards Addressed: Reading for Information 1, 2, 10)

Assignment: *Students are to create a test* on the story of Wilma Rudolph. Four to seven of the questions can be student-chosen, any kind of question they want: fill in the blank, multiple choice. But they must ask one good "Why?" question, for critical thinking purposes. You may add your own questions here as well, in sensitivity to your students. Let everyone know that the next day, you will read selective questions aloud for them to vote on for the final test. Emphasize that *yes, they will be making up their own test and taking it!*

After taking and reviewing the co-created test, follow by asking the students to volunteer any recapitulation of the lessons on attention. What is good to learn? Clue them to include:

• Every time you practice giving attention, you are making your mound a bit bigger; and you are exercising your attention muscle. Your mound grows bigger and your attention muscle gets stronger.

• It takes a really, really long time of exercising your attention muscle, but when you can concentrate and focus with excellence, a "magic door" appears. For you can do almost anything you set yourself to do. With an excellence of attention greatness can come.

Discussion Items to be considered about the development of attention:

—*giving* and *paying* attention as different from being *entertained* or *getting* stimulated; lead them to compare and observe the differences with *focusing, relaxing*, and *zombie-eyed* (at a screen).

—discuss the "magic door" of *excellent attention*, the power of excellence, like being in 'the zone', or a time when you couldn't miss, or the special feeling of doing your best;

—invite corroboration about how watching *too much* TV softens the attention muscle. (Perhaps you can explain how the word *entertain* and *attention* are related (*tendere*, to stretch). It could be said that "entertain" implies *being held* (or the relaxing the "stretch" of attention), whereas "attention" implies the actual "stretch" made in holding. The muscle of attention grows by stretching and holding, then rests in being held.) Some "Screen Time" is good and healthy, too much will make you weak and sick.

Generate examples of attention-building activities that are superior to all the glowing screens. Examples include: building models, making things, cooking, playing chess, playing cards, playing ping pong, etc. Invite the kids into the self-generated process of building their own attention muscle.

Recite!

I give all my children small prizes to those who can recite the recitation below aloud, multiple attempts are accepted. (That way it is heard about ~30 times.) Naturally, you will want to explore what it means to "learn to lose." Have the children talk about the feelings surrounding failure and how being honest about feelings helps you to persist. I also have this quote as a small poster in the front of my room.

Recitation

"Winning is great, sure, but if you are going to do something in life, *the secret is learning how to lose.* Nobody goes undefeated all the time. If you can pick yourself up after a defeat, and go on to win again, you can be a champion."

— Wilma Rudolph

Writing Response:

Discuss the accomplishment of a poor sick girl who was not suppose to live or walk. Ask the children to remember when the doctors told her that she would never walk again. Ask them to imagine going from her *challenging* situation to world-excellence. What did Wilma say was the secret?

"My Mom's (Dad's, caregiver's) Heroism". Have the children relay the story of Wilma Rudolph to a caregiver as best as they can. Then they are to **interview that adult** about a time they learned this lesson of persistence through failure and accomplished something difficult. Examples are: getting an educational degree, climbing a mountain, having a baby, getting a particular job, learning to paint or play music, etc.

The children can use any or all of the following questions to help with their interview:

•What was one of the hardest things you've ever done?

•Where were you living?

•Did you want to give up? Tell me about it.

•Were you afraid you couldn't do it? Tell me how you felt.

•How old were you?

•What were your expectations? What happened?

•How did you feel when you were done?

•How would you describe the lesson of persistence you learned that helped you later?

Based on notes from the interview, the students are to **write** the story for the teacher (and since they are private, they will not be shared without permission), telling their teacher about **someone in their life who did something very hard**.

Here, I only require minimal revision, according to the tenor of my students, for the emphasis on praise, voice, and excitement should be maximized. But before the story is turned in, the adult-interviewed is to read the story, add suggestions, clarifications or elaborations, (and perhaps a couple of grammatical points?) and then the child is to <u>rewrite</u> the story, incorporating those improvements. Here you *begin* to teach (but not yet fulfill): "Writing IS re-writing." Right away, I begin a call-response, "Writing IS....." and they chorus back, "RE-writing!" I repeat this throughout the year.

I review paragraph construction (a la "Basic Cheeseburger", topic sentence+) and basic grammar requirements (see Five Finger Review p. 61). I teach my students how to use this writing assessment as a 'dip-stick' assessment.

As the beginning writing piece in my school, I accept all submissions that are re-written at least once. We'll introduce full-scale editing and the five-step writing process soon. For now, all submissions are heartily praised and many end up being shared. Often the parent is the heroine or hero of the story, instantly integrating home and school.

*****

Taking it to heart: Self-Challenges
Tie the "Attention Muscle" to Distraction Management
and Personal Academic Achievement

Quick Write: Engage the children in a discussion on distraction management; talk about the difficulty of focusing at length on tasks, how different distractions are present at home and school. Have the children consider at least one school task (and one 'non-academic' task) that they want to work on getting better and why they chose that subject (e.g. multiplication facts, handwriting, paragraph writing, et cetera). Guide them to create a list of distractions or difficulties they might encounter. Work with them to co-create and fill in their "charts of improvement".

I want to get better at	Now I can do	I bet I can	I'll talk about it with	Distractions? Obstacles?	Timeline? % of Goal Reached

Possible Follow-up: More *Core Stories*

Have the children read the other *Core Stories* on Attention, and then write a Compare-Contrast analysis of one or two other stories. Have a class discussion on favorite features of the different stories. This will provide ample opportunity to repeat and reinforce the affective strengths addressed in this lesson.

Follow-up: Simple Self-Observation: Personal Timeline

At this point, in order to serve self-observation and the growth of attention, I have the students make a personal timeline (with their caretakers help) as below, focusing on events and things they learned to do. This homework assignment naturally integrates a host of standards, while personal challenges and growth are naturally cultivated.

1. Have the students make a Timeline, starting with the year of their birth. Give them one sheet of paper for each year they have been alive.
2. Fold each paper in half, top to bottom, open back up and draw a line across the crease. Have them write "1" in the first top left corner of the first page, "2" on the second page, etc.
3. Review basic "scale mathematics": for instance, in delineating their birthday on page one of the timeline, where would it be on the first sheet? (January 1, far left; December 31, far right). We see from this exercise that each year could easily be divided into twelve parts.
4. *On the top half* of each paper, the students are to write down a significant event or two from each year of <u>their</u> life or their home life, graphing it on the timeline in chronological order (add pictures too, as student below did.) *On the bottom half* of each paper, the children are to write any significant social events that happened outside their family. (They do this for homework, and the children get elder input.)
5. Have your students tape these sheets together *chronologically*, making their own timeline.

   After the students get input from home on things that happened in their life (that they want to share!) Collect and evaluate the basic writing skills of your students. Have your students share in appropriate ways. Note the commonalities in personal and social notations. *Save this work* for their autobiographies they will soon write.

Benicia with her Timeline (Taitiana helping)

Teaching Restraint: "Start/Stop"

I also specifically teach **restraint** and what the phrase "holding back on the reins" means. I tell my fifth grade class that *it is one of the main life skills they must learn*. I tell them of the famous Walter Mischel marshmellow study and ask them to predict the resuts. Feel free to re-create it!

A first grade teacher at my school teaches restraint with the game "Start-Stop". Her children must learn to **Start** an activity, then on signal, **Stop** it. Make it silly at first!

I **extend** this exercise of restraint to my fifth grade students with the quick and wild version of "Start/Stop". First, I tell my fifth graders that they will soon be teen-agers and in a few years will probably be driving and maybe kissing (moans) ... and if they don't know how to put on the brakes as well as the gas, well, a crash will happen.

I ask the children if they could be both wild AND restrained at the same time. My infamous and student-enjoyable method is to have a *modified* paper-wad fight in class! Here are the rules:

1. It must be SILENT.
2. No super-hard throws/face hitting.
3. It must be fun, no meanies!
4. Upon my Signal, absolutely STOP (or never again?)
5. There must be a silent clean-up by volunteers.

Everyone agrees? If anyone violates any of the rules, it's OVER. I usually let it go for about a minute (and join in) and if everyone follows the happy and learning nature of the activity, I announce that we'll do it again some other time. Every time, I repeat the rules and the reason for the activity: we're learning restraint! Start-Stop!

*****

Studenthood Report Card

Use the following "Studenthood Report Card" as a follow-up to the whole unit. Review each portion and explain the meaning of each portion. Let them know you think highly of them already, but everyone knows there is room for improvement. The students can fill it out themselves OR they can take it home and mutually fill out the report card with any chosen adult. Using Report Card as a prompt, parent and child can discuss areas of strength and at least one area that needs improvement. It is a great self-reflection for the children on how they can improve their attention and a useful way to connect the home and school settings.

This "report card" (see following two pages) provides another strong link in the home-school connection. It can help create a "culture of expectation", wherein trying is universally valued and expected.

Teacher: _____

Parent Signature: _____

Response Letter from Student/Parent? ☐ / ☐

Name _____

Studenthood Report Card _____

(Date)

1.0 Trying (Overall)

1.1 Understands the process of trying, application, and challenge.

1.2 Is seen applying herself/himself
    In most areas:
    In some areas:

1.3 Asks Questions and Participates in Class:

2.0 Understands the Features of Attention

2.1 Can communicate the feelings associated with failure.

2.15 Understands that temporary defeats are part of the task.

2.2 Fully Understands the Words: **"Persist", "Focus", "Concentrate".**

2.3 Understands the difference between getting attention and giving attention.

3.0 Restraint (Overall)

3.1 Understands "Start-Stop"

3.2 Demonstrates Listening

3.3 Demonstrates Commitment to Excellence Beyond Distractions

LEGEND

1–10
(with 10 = awesome)
5 = average)

Comments

Notes for Parents/Caregivers

This is the Overall Grade.

Does your child understand that paying attention is a muscle that one develops over time?

*This takes into account shyness **and other factors**, but is still very important.*

This examines the features and meanings of attention building. Can your child tell you about these?

This is the Overall Grade.

"Start-Stop" is the capacity to go from free time to focus, from talking to paying attention.

Talk with your child about "excellence" and distractions.

☐ *Please note under the teacher's and parent's signatures, there is place to check ✓ if you wish to write to the teacher or have your child write about their commitment to their education.*

1.0 <u>Trying</u>

1.1 Understands the <u>process</u> of trying, application, and challenge.

1.2 Is seen applying herself/himself
In most areas:
In some areas:

1.3 Asks Questions and Participates in Class:

2.0 <u>Understands the Features of Attention</u>

2.1 Can communicate the feelings associated with failure.

2.15 Understands that temporary defeats are part of the task.

2.2 Fully Understands the Words:
"Persist", "Focus", "Concentrate".

3.0 <u>Restraint</u>

3.1 Understands "Start-Stop"

3.2 Demonstrates Listening

3.3 Demonstrates Commitment to Excellence Beyond Distractions

---

STUDENTHOOD

Report Card

_____
Student

_____
School

_____
date

Unit Two: Tell Me a Story
Children Practice Self-Expression While Exercising the Features of Story-Telling

From Across the Parking Lot to My Fun Story

The Legend of English

Autobiographical Frames

Retelling Fairy Tales

Common Core Standards Addressed: <u>Writing</u> Narratives 3a, b, d, e; 4, 5, 10

<u>Speaking and Listening</u>: 1 b, c Collaboration

<u>Reading Informational Text</u>: 5, 6

Tell Me a Story

Story-creation literally and artistically lets students express their own feelings in their own terms, in ways they want to see. This emotional expressiveness is very attractive to them ... you just require a bit of framework and a few ways to improve it.

Here we focus on the **fundamentals of story**: Main Idea, Setting, Character, and Plot. Intentionally pedantic, intentionally interactive, and explicitly requiring artist illustrations, here we teach beginning editing and repeated rewriting... all the while we help them make their story shine.

<u>**Main Idea**</u> **- Activity**

Warm up Activity for the Main Idea: Challenge volunteers *to say in less than one breath* what some common stories are about: e.g., *Jack and the Beanstalk, Cinderella, Star Wars*, any popular cartoon/entertainment show, etc. Guide the children to use fewer and fewer words. This will take some guidance and many examples. Once they demonstrate a <u>basic</u> capacity to summarize a story in one breath, tell them this *main idea* also could be called the "Set Up"--or even the *title* of the story. Review the *subtitle* of books and movies.

Once you have exercised the main idea of traditional or common tales, ask the children to imagine that they find a short story that would love to read. In a dream or a crystal ball or a vision, they see the book in their hands. This story would be just the kind of funny or scary or exciting story that they would like to read about. Now ask them to imagine that they look at the story and it is written by them! Their name is on it! They can't wait to open it, but before they can "turn the page", they must learn how to make a good title and then three parts of a story.

Write: Ask the children to **imagine** that they accidently see a famous movie producer across a parking lot. The producer looks up at their hopeful eyes and guesses, "You have a story you think would be a great movie, right? OK, what is it about?" Remember, it has to be <u>in one breath</u>. What do they yell? Have your children **write** that down.

As they are writing, remind them that this is the "Set Up" and Main Idea.

Next: **Imagine** : Luck is with them. The next day they get into an elevator and hit number 23 when the same producers steps in and hits 22. He recognizes you and says, "That was a good story idea. You have until the elevator lets me off to tell me more."

Talk & Art: Children pair up and **tell** their partner their expanded story for **one minute. Listeners** are encouraged to ask questions to help story-tellers elaborate or clarify. After both partners have talked their story, then each child quickly illustrates/sketches at least one picture in their own story (**pictures** first; many students will love the opportunity to **draw first**). Tell them they have a ten? minutes deadline for their **sketch**, and graciously allowing them more, but *motion* here is key. Students explain their picture(s) to their partner for one minute each. Each student asks their fellow questions. Now each student explains the story again in only sixty seconds!

Write: Have each student then write the elevator version of their story. Encourage continued partner corroboration, partner sharing, adding, questioning. Fifteen-twenty minute deadline. As your students write, <u>give them the following condition of engagement</u>: No erasing! If they mess up or don't like something, they draw a ~~single line through it~~, but keep it and keep going. Tell them this is what writers often do. Developing this technique will spare many frustrations, and help the students **keep it moving**.

One of my fellows and friends, Dan Alderson, says to his students, "One word and then another word and another. One word at a time." (He gives points for words and that sum is a major component of their grade.) Keep it moving... As they write, encourage them to write, not think... "think aloud, that is, write aloud". Yes, be a cheerleader.

After the time is up, share, praise, and inquire. For homework, they are to read their one-minute- story writing aloud to an elder. Elaboration and input from elders should be **written down** along with any further elaborations (or re-writes!).

Setting Game: Where am I?   *(thanks to Anne Diskin for this game)*

Writing preparation: The Teacher passes out 3x5 cards and asks the children to name a place on one side, like "bus stop" or "lunchroom" or "my room", then add their name. <u>On the other side</u> neatly write at least two things they see there. Thirty seconds later, ask them to name a sound they might hear (write); fifteen seconds later, smells or sensations (at least four entries altogether).

As they are writing, draw a face on the board and, then ask for volunteers to give examples of their sensory descriptions. As they do so, point to the facial correlative and indicate the sensations/senses they are including (eye for sight, nose for smell, ears for hearing, mouth for taste, and I use the cheek for "touch"). Use the words "sensory" and "senses" with "description" and "sensation".

After they write down their clues, the cards are collected and randomly redistributed, **clues side up** (no peaking on the other side). Students are selected to read the clues and guess the <u>place</u> (others can guess/concur afterwards). Kudos will be naturally affored to the student who *wrote* the excellent clues.

Tell the children they just learned one of the basics for the foundational lesson of writing: **Setting**. Tell them there are only a few parts to learn to make a great story and if you learn the parts of a story, it is easy to build one.

Note: First, teach Setting <u>only</u> and then take only the setting through the writing process itself. Sketch, Write, Improve, Rewrite, and Show— **all for the Setting only**. This way the weaker writers are not overwhelmed with writing and rewriting and rewriting. Simply take the two to four sentences they have constructed for SetUp and Setting through the writing process. This will be an abbreviated and easy form of the writing process. But it communicates clearly one key lesson about writing: it is a *process*.

The children will write their imagined story, using their "Set-Up"/main idea and Setting. Remind they that they will be writing the story that they would love to hear. (Later, you will talk about "audience".)

Tell the children there are three big parts of a story to learn: the **Setting**, the **Characters** and the **Plot**. It's good for beginners to start with **Setting,** leading the reader visualize and feel the story. There are many ingredients in a Setting, so let's start with the basics.

Tell the children to imagine a story and answer the questions on the Set-Up / Setting Prewrite below; tell them that pre-writes are one good way to begin to sketch out a story. Remind them they already did do a prewrite with the 3x5 card-game. Tell them they must first focus on the FIRST scene in their story. Ask: what place is story taking place?

Adaptation for my students in the second and third grades, I would simple ask them to imagine a scene and they had to tell me and write:

1. Time of the day (morning, after lunch, after school, midnight, etc.)
2. Season or time of the year (Halloween night, Kwanzaa Feast, first day of the summer, etc.)
3. Two things seen
4. One thing heard
5. One "extra" detail: temperature, smell, taste, ??
6. A feeling, an emotion.

Set-Up and Setting   (PreWrite)

1) Parking Lot Yell/**Main Idea**/Big Set-up (This *could* be the **Title**):

What is your story about — can you say it in one breath? (Could be the Title of the Story or a full breath description.)

_____

_____

2) **Where** does the first scene take place?_____

(Your room? On your neighborhood streets? The moons of Jupiter? A dream?)

3) **What time of day** or night is it? _____

(Dawn? Lunchtime? Afterschool? After bedtime?)

4) **What time of the year** is it? _____

(Springtime? Holidays? Dark Winter?)

5) **What 2-3 things can be seen**?

_____

_____

(Wind on the trees? Sunlight on the water? People doing what?)

6) **What sounds do can be heard**?_____

7) **What smells or tastes are there**? _____

8) **What feelings are there**? _____ / _____

(smooth, rough   /   happy, sad)

outside   /   *inside*

The Writing Process
(in discrete, small pieces)

Write (Idealistic Teacher Prompt): "Take the answers from your pre-write and **write** your notes into complete sentences (reviewing the need for capitalization, punctuation, and subject-verb agreement). This first writing is called a 'draft' or a sloppy copy. 'Draft' means a 'pretend (or preliminary) version' so don't worry about mistakes or spelling or anything really, just put down one word at a time, making as good sentences as you can. Read it all out loud to yourself, seeing how it sounds, checking for big mistakes. Rewrite it better. Then, if you can, read that first re-write aloud to someone.

"Now the bad news: you have to do it again. Introduce the first big skill: **blending the sentences**. Blend the sentences as best as you can, don't worry about getting it "right" or "finished". For instance, you would **not** write: *It was my happiest day. I was at the beach. It was sunset. It was summer. I saw waves, clouds, and people playing frisbee. I heard the waves, birds, and people yelling. I smelled bar-b-que. I felt hungry and happy.*

First Blend: *It was sunset on the beach, one happy summer day. I saw waves and heard them. Birds chirped and flew through the smell of bar-b-ques. People were yelling and I was hungry and excited.*

"**Now a really hard part** for some people: *don't write any more than this.* No, 'then a shark or a man jumped out of the water', or 'there was a party we wanted to go to', no 'I met this fun person who...'. Nothing else! It may be **two long sentences or four, but it is short.** We'll work on **just this** 'Setting' introduction and make it great. By keeping it short, we only have to work on making it good with a two or three sentences."

• Remind everyone that the **writing process is a series of re-writes**, like a potter making a vase: craft, adjust, craft, adjust, smooth, color, fire.

Write: After your first draft, **improve it simply.** The **first** and easiest thing to do is to **add adjectives** and **adverbs**. Find all your nouns and see if there's an adjective that would work, then find all your verbs and see if they could use any adverb or adverbial phrase.

It was just before sunset on the city beach on a warm summer day. I saw and heard big waves crashing loudly; I heard nearby birds chirping loudly and flying fast through the smokes of supper bar-b-ques. That made me hungry. People were yelling loudly and I was very happy.

Just this little decorating and our paragraph is already way better.

Another easy way to improve a paragraph is to use a Thesaurus. Find overused words like "big" or "loud", "very" or <u>any main word that is used more than once per paragraph.</u>

It was just before sunset on the beach, one warm summer day. I saw huge waves crashing and heard their thunderous roar, while nearby birds chirped sharply and flew quickly through the smell of supper bar-b-ques. That made me hungry! People were yelling with excitement and I was rushing with happiness.

I don't ask for too much <u>at first</u>, according to my population and my style. I let three re-writes be enough to publish in this onset of the curriculum.

According to the style and art of your teaching: praise profusely; approve each one and tell them they are ready to "Publish".

Publish

I ceremoniously reveal some 11" x 17" paper. I fold it in half, left-to-right, open it back up and tell the children to rewrite their finished-words in their best handwriting anywhere on the open sheet. They can write their words on one side, top or bottom, or across the whole bottom, that's up to them. Then they draw a picture of what the words are saying, stick figures are fine. No exceptions, all must try and illustrate. First write the words, then make an illustration. When they are done, they will have the first page of their book. (The cover is put on last. Instructions for assembly later.)

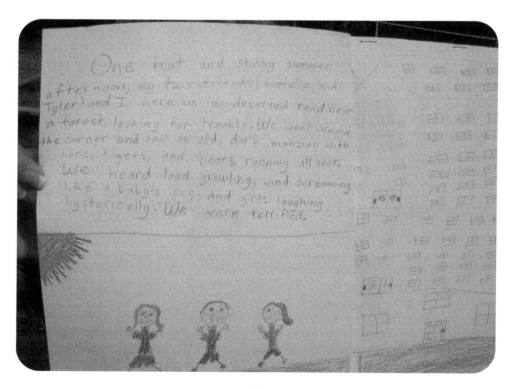

Their theatrical play protesting candy cigarettes made the local newspaper.

A Character Appears

Tell the kids for their next page they have a **character** appear: a friend, a stranger, a magical being, a villain — that's up to them. Use the accompanying pre-write sheet (below) to talk about ways to describe a character (point out that this is a **brainstorming tool** and they will probably NOT use every detail). However, emphasize to the learners that they must note the character's <u>wants</u> and <u>fears</u>.

Likewise, take these prewrite sentences through the writing process (to the degree your students can), ending in Publish! exactly like *Setting*. I find that by taking a paragraph or less through the writing process, it is easier to learn and improve. Bite-sized pieces are sweet.

Desire and Plot

After the Character prewrite, draft, rewrites, and publishing, we begin our Plot lesson. Begin with what the character <u>wants</u>— which is the beginning of the Plot Prewrite. Plot is only "conflict" when there has first been desire. Something happens to interfere with the desire of the character: That is the structure of "conflict". Examples are: they have no money, or they hear about a party, but ....

Clarify: The Character pre-write *ends* and the *Plot* pre-write *begins* with **desire** (which is *then* conflicted). Clarify: "What does the character want? and fear?" This desire drives the story of problems and solutions. Wants have conflicts, goals, and fears: desire is first.

Next: Have the learners note the "rising action" and the "climax" places on the Plot Prewrite and teach this rising excitement by tone and example. In every new scene, they are to sensually describe the setting and any new character.

Take the Character and Plot paragraphs through similar revisions. Be sure to have the children illustrate them.

After you have "approved" each of their rewrites, they illustrate it and affix the Setting paragraph/illustration together with the *Character* paragraph/illustration. The Plot page follows in like fashion. I then staple/glue them all together so that the pages "turn", adding any further pages the same way: (V+V+V). Finish by having them draw an illustrated cover and back page wrapping around everything else.

They made their own book! Everyone is very proud. I usually make a hallway bulletin board out of it, affixing only the last page so that other students can read them hanging there. I save these creations for the caregivers/parents on back to school night.

Character Prewrite

Person: _____/_____/_____/_____
           Gender   **Age**   **Name**   **Body shape/size**

Hair: Color? _____ **Cut?** _____ **Condition?** _____

Clothes: Color? _____ **Style?** _____ **Condition?** _____

Eyes Seem to be Saying: _____

Action: Is Doing _____

Saying/Body Language: _____

*Wants/Desires _____ ***Is Afraid of:** _____

How would they respond to:

What's up?/How's it going?

It's raining ...

Do you like _____?

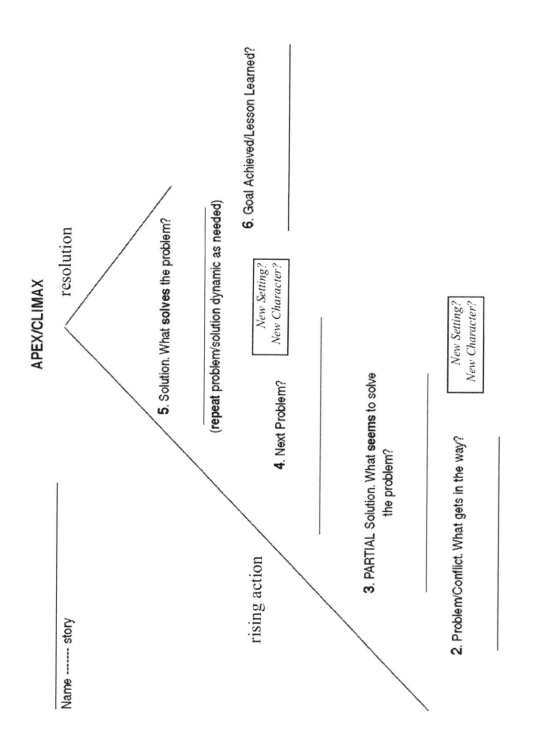

Name ------- story

APEX/CLIMAX

resolution

rising action

1. DESIRE. What does the character WANT?

2. Problem/Conflict. What gets in the way?

New Setting?
New Character?

3. PARTIAL Solution. What **seems** to solve the problem?

4. Next Problem?

New Setting?
New Character?

(repeat problem/solution dynamic as needed)

5. Solution. What **solves** the problem?

6. Goal Achieved/Lesson Learned?

PLOT PREWRITE

Writing: My Halloween Story
(Optional, 1-2 weeks)

Having learned the fundamentals of story creation in the school year's beginning, they can make their own Halloween story/booklet is kid-exciting way to practice the main idea, setting, character, plot. But now we introduce the concept of coloring the words, using three levels of description: "Plain, Silver, and Golden" sentence. In the next lesson, we will develop and focus on Coloring the Words, so this is a brief introduction. Briefly, to "Silverize" a sentence, add adjectives, adverbs, and sensory descriptions. To make a sentence "Golden", we use Similes, Metaphors, Hyperbole, and Personification. Emphasize that good paragraphs often have *all three kinds* of sentences. (See the larger, reproducible chart on page 63.)

Plain, Silver, and Golden Sentences

1. **Plain** -- says a LITTLE clearly! Every writing needs short sentences. <u>Every communication needs some simple sayings</u>, but most plain sentences need to be enriched.

> e.g. "She had black hair."
> "He was nice."
> "We stopped."

2. **Silver** -- says MORE. Find the nouns and add adjectives, find the verbs consider adverbs;

> e.g. "He was friendly and happy."
> "She had black, shiny hair."
> "We stopped abruptly."

3. GOLDEN -- says it ALL! Use similes, metaphors, personification, hyperbole, alliteration.

> e.g. "He was so kind, his heart lighted the room."
> "Her long, black hair was so fine, the sun glistened off of it in sheets of light."
> "We stopped so abruptly I thought my eyeballs would pop out."

The best writings have all three: plain, silver and golden.

After you have challenged your students to write samples of silver and golden sentences, have them share. Praise exceptional adjectives and antonyms, applaud figurative language. Then use these paragraphs to teach the rubric self-assessment (p. 64) for their own evaluation of their writing. Have them grade themselves and submit their own rubric when they turn in writing pieces.

Teacher Preparation for "The Legend of English"

Warm up: Tell the children that every thing can be characterized as having a beginning, a development, and eventually, an end. (And that end is often the stuff of new beginnings.) Flowers are "first" sprouted seeds, etc.... Ask for two examples. The story of that beginning, development, and end is called the "history" of any thing.

Then tell them that even languages have a history. A famous language, Latin, the language of the Romans for over a thousand years and for another thousand years with the smarty-pants of Europe, is now a "dead" language, (but there are thousands and thousands of words in English that come from Latin. Since I teach in California, I often digress and talk about "Latino", explaining that the Spanish kids in my class already know lots of Latin and that by knowing Spanish they have a special strength). Tell them that they are going to learn something that most grown-ups don't know: how "English" came to be. Tell them that knowing this story will give them a power like they could pull a sword out of stone.

1) Have the students make a timeline that stretches from 44 BCE to the present. I distribute paper rolls in ~4' lengths and instruct/demonstrate to them the marking in scale. Tell them you will make a few marks on the timeline together, then as they read the story, they can make other demarcations.

   Demonstrate and instruct them in delineating -44, 0, 500, 1000, 1500, 2000, 416, 1066, 1609, 1776, 1969, 2000, and the current year.

Have the students make their first mark on the extreme left side of their timeline and label it 44BCE. **Ask** if anyone knows what BCE means. You will probably have to **explain** the evolution of BC and AD into BCE and CE. Then, use your pull-down map to show Rome, the extent of the Roman Empire and Britain, and explain:

"The Roman Empire spread order and writing across the Western World. They built excellent roads and protected them so people could enjoy widespread commerce (what does this word mean? yes, like "commercial"); they built ships and protected the seas, spreading order and growing stronger and bigger all the time. Sometimes the were smart and kind and sometimes they were mean and selfish, but they usually brought order.

"One of the things the Romans needed was the metal *tin*, which, when melted with copper, makes an **alloy**, or mixture of metals, of *bronze*. Bronze is *much* stronger than regular copper (why would this be important? I usually pause here and talk about the disadvantages of copper saws in cutting stones for the Egyptian pyramids). In "minus 44", or 44BCE, the Roman Army established one of their grand encampments on the Thames river, named for a Celtic leader, *Londonium,* here." [Point to map of England and indicate the mouth of the Thames.]

Warm up: Tell them they "will learn that English is cool in that it is made up basically of four languages: very old German, ancient Latin, old French, and ancient Greek. When you learn English, you learn four languages at once! There are other languages inside English too, but those four make up almost all of it. That's why English is so strong. *It has the strengths of four languages.* It can be very exact and beautifully poetic, strikingly simple and brilliantly intellectual, dear and sweet and strong while being elegant, eloquent, and clear.

"English wasn't always around. The four languages merged together over time. How German, French, Latin, and Greek came together is the history of English.

"Think about it. This language wasn't always around. This is the legend of how English came to be, grew up, and became very powerful."

Review with them how to pre-view a reading. Tell them that one of the secrets of understanding is knowing your words *really well*. What's one of the secrets of understanding?

Have the students go over the following **glossary** (words that were collected by my fifth-grade English Learners), read all the definitions, see the blanks. Tell them that their job is to finish the glossary, but they can find many of the words defined in the story. In addition, the students should **skim** the following pages and **create** a class list of problem words and questions. Go over what they find.

Tell the children that they will learn about 4,000 new words this year! You will teach them maybe a thousand and their family and friends will teach them another thousand, and how do they think they will learn the other 2,000? Themselves! By reading! Tell them that learning the story of English will supercharge their ability to understand words.

Vocabulary Development and Preparation for *The Legend of English*

(some words are defined, others are defined in the story, some need elaboration or research)

legend: a famous or great story, mostly or probably true.

tin: a metal _____

decade: ten years

metropolis: BIG city.

alloy: when metals _____

brass: _____

Brittons, Wales, Scotland (Review the Map: Britain and the Continent)

Frisians, Angles, Saxons, Jutes (see enclosed maps)

invaded: _____

thorough(ly): _____

Beowulf: A story over a thousand years old, written in the Old English style.

Vikings, Norse, Scandinavian (review on map)

Normans: the Northmen or "Norseman" who invaded, then settled into the French north shore.

discourse: talking back and forth

Britain: what the original Celts called their land, now including England, Wales, and Scotland.

bilingualism: speaking two languages

Canterbury: the center of religion in England.

Renaissance: the _____ of Greek ideas and intellectual freedom.

resurgence: _____

philosophical: "love of wisdom", thinking deeply about things.

Shakespeare: _____

reinherited: got it back again; received again that which is yours.

intellectual: Thinking deeply about ideas.

Romance languages (sprouted from Rome's Latin: French, Italian, Spanish, Portuguese, Romanian)

poetic: like poetry, like you were there

rational: makes sense

The Legend of English

Pre-Read Questions: Why did Rome want to conquer Britannia? What language did the Romans speak across their empire? After the Romans left, who invaded Britannia? English is made up mainly from what FOUR languages?

Over two thousand years ago, the biggest empire in the Western world was the Roman Empire. They needed to make lots of the hard metal called brass, which is made by melting softer copper (like in pennies or electric wire) and soft tin together, making a hard alloy. While the Romans had lots of copper, they didn't have much tin.

The Extent of the Roman Empire before taking Britannia

Britannia were famous for its tin. So in 44BCE, or minus 44, the Romans under Julius Caesar established a military camp at *Londonium*, what we now call_____. Over the next decade or so, the Romans finally drove the Celtic Brittons west into the lands we now call Wales and north into the lands we call Scotland, giving the mighty Romans full access to the tin they needed. We retain almost no Celtic in English, save the sweet-sounding names of towns and rivers.

For over four hundred years, Latin was spoken in Roman-ized Britain (as well as in the rest of the West). It was the language of business, education, and politics. But an overpopulation of Germans combined with a prolonged corruption in Roman politics and the Empire began to fall apart. Rome withdrew its troops from Brittania in the year 406, and in 476, the huge viaducts that feed the ancient metropolis fresh water were destroyed. Without water, the great metropolis shrank to a large village very quickly. Rome was then easily overrun by the German Vandals, Visigoths, and other "barbarians".

Imagine what it would be like if suddenly there were no police, no army, no widespread order. [**Discussion**: how would this affect: business, education, <u>food choices</u>, arts, safety, +?]

The next five hundred years lacked wide-spread order, growth, and education so badly that it was called "The Dark Ages."

After the withdrawal of Roman soldiers, Britain was supposedly ruled for a generation by the legendary Arturo, King Arthur. But after Arturo, there was not a sufficient coalition of Celtic fighters and so the old Roman Britannia was successfully invaded by the West Germanic tribes of Angles (or Engles), Saxons, and Jutes, and by the Dutch Frisians. These Germanic dialects partially merged in Britannia and became known as *Englisc*.

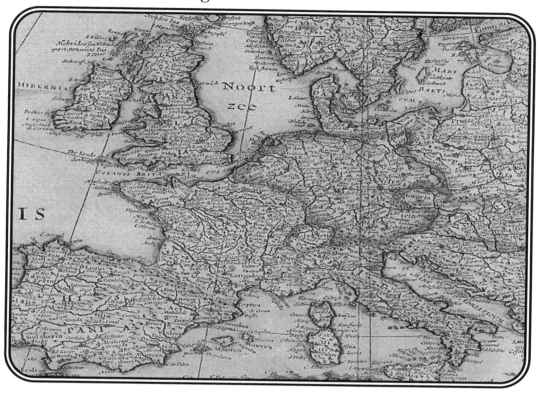

Soon thereafter, Christian missionaries returned the Latin alphabet to Britain, displacing the Scandinavian system of lettering, but the spoken language remained thoroughly Germanic. The "Anglo-Saxons" defended Britain (Engles'-land) against the Vikings for several hundred years, developing their own dialect. These Dark Ages were the time of Old English.

> [Note: Looking at the chart, **The Body of English** (p. 53), *we see*
> "GERMANIC" *is written across the trunk. This is a metaphor to say
> that the Germanic tongues is the trunk of our language. Thus we
> inherit from the Old English:* "**mind, brain, body, hands, eyes, ears,
> nose, mouth, soul, house, rooms, doors, windows, street, place,
> worked, played, spoke, ran, leaped...**".]

Beowulf's Kingly adventures were written at the end of this period. Old English looks and sounds like: meaning:

Hwæt!	*Listen!*
We Gardena	*We of the Spear-Danes*
þeodcyninga in geardagum,	*in the old days and we heard of their glory*
hu ua æpelingas	*how these noble warriors.*
ellen fremedon.	*performed courageous deeds.*

A little over a thousand years ago, the Vikings began swarming out of Scandinavia. They took over Greenland, Iceland, founded a colony in Newfoundland, re-attacked England again, and took over the north of France. In France, they settled in nicely, married wonderful French women and within a generation were all speaking French, though they passed on many words from Norse (*Tuesday, Wednesday, Thursday, Friday*).

Bayeux Tapestry Illustrating the Norman Conquest

Then in the year 1066, the Norman (Northmen=Norseman=Norman) Conquest of England brought copious amounts of French, Latin and Norse into English, especially in the Royal Court and government, sweetening the rougher Germanic discourse.

[Note: Looking at the wall-chart, **The Body of English** on page 53, we see French is written across the throat. This is a metaphor to say that French sweetened the sound of Old German. "A Journey of Surrender, a Royal Labour of Courage..."]

As the Vikings were finally controlled by the rise of the castles and knights, the West faced a new invasion from the south and East: the advancing Muslims. Christian Europe fought back the invading armies of Islam and decided to use their knights to counter-attack and re-take Jerusalem. For two hundred years (1095-1291), the "Crusades" fought for the "Holy Land" and, while the final outcome was a stalemate, the real treasure was found in wagonloads of books they brought back. This knowledge, combined with a stable Europe, ended the Dark Ages.

In Britain during the eleven-hundreds, bilingualism (speaking both French and English) became common, but in 1204, the English kings lost Normandy to the French and England began to re-establish English as the official language. But by now, the sweet French had infused rougher English with thousands of words, both French and Latin. This sweetening time was the period of "Middle English". English began to have three words for many, many things; the "triplets" from Old English, Old French, and Old Latin. For example, *kingly/royal/regal, ask/question/interrogate, fast/firm/secure, holy/sacred/consecrated, work/labour/exertion*, etc.

The greatest writer of the Middle English period was the great poet Geoffrey Chaucer. He wrote a book called *Canterbury Tales* (in the year 1380) that made fun of almost everybody and was written in the most beautiful speech that had ever appeared in English. Unfortunately, the sound of all the vowels has changed so much that it is hard to appreciate the literary brilliance any more. Please visit with your class Canterbury Tales online for translation and to hear it spoken.

1: Whan that aprill with his shoures soote
2: The droghte of march hath perced to the roote,
3: And bathed every veyne in swich licour
4: Of which vertu engendred is the flour;
5: Whan zephirus eek with his sweete breeth
6: Inspired hath in every holt and heeth
7: Tendre croppes, and the yonge sonne
8: Hath in the ram his halve cours yronne,
9: And smale foweles maken melodye,
10: That slepen al the nyght with open ye

Thus, English at this time was half rooted in the Germanic languages (German, Norse, Scandinavian) and half in the Romance languages (French and

Latin), and so we find **The Body of English** to have a "German" trunk framed by the "Romance" languages -- French throat and arms, Latin legs.

In 1454, the printing press announced the time known as the "Renaissance" or "rebirth" of widespread knowledge. Europe was reborn as it re-inherited the wisdom of the ancient Greeks and the re-inspiration of intellectual inquiry. This rebirth had many repercussions; including the resurgence of scientific and philosophical thought and, in English, the Great Vowel Shift of the Sixteenth Century, announcing the end of Middle English. Nobody really knows why, but in the middle part of the 1500's the vowels all changed. It was like the short vowels became long and the long became short.

Now, in addition to *Englisc*, Old French, and more Latin, ancient Greek was stirred in. As they all melted together a new, powerful language appeared: Modern English is strong and supple, sweet and exact, poetic and logical, practical and abstract, feeling and philosophical.

Upon this new stage, the genius Shakespeare stepped forth (about 1600) to show the glory and power of many languages at once. Nowadays, most people can't read Old English or Middle English, but we can start understanding historical English starting around the time of Shakespeare. It sounds weird or funny, and lots of words need to be explained, but even kids can get it.

All the world's a stage,
And all the men and women merely players;
They have their exits and their entrances;
And one man in his time plays many parts,
His acts being seven ages. At first the infant,
Mewling and puking in the nurse's arms;
Then the whining school-boy, with his satchel
And shining morning face, creeping like snail
Unwillingly to school. And then the lover,
Sighing like furnace, with a woeful ballad
Made to his mistress' eyebrow. Then a soldier,
Full of strange oaths, and bearded like the pard,
Jealous in honour, sudden and quick in quarrel,
Seeking the bubble reputation ....

> *Last scene of all,*
> *That ends this strange eventful history,*
> *Is second childishness and mere oblivion;*
> *Sans teeth, sans eyes, sans taste, sans everything.*

As the Greek wisdom tradition was reinherited, it infused English with a developed brilliance and logical insistence, and we find that our intellectual concepts and newly created words are often Greek. Thus, looking at **The Body of English**, the logical head thinks and speaks most often in Greek. From Greek we get *democracy, philosophy, theater, mathematics, school, athletics, therapy, skeptical, music, authentic, paradoxical, logical ....*

This melding of Germanic, Romance and Greek languages began the period of Modern English, which rode upon the decks of the expanding British Empire to affect and be affected by a host of other languages around the world.

Thus, English has the largest vocabulary of any language and draws strengths and subtleties from many tongues: it is the world-language of science, travel, business, diplomacy, and aviation.

Knowing this history will make you stronger and help you learn new words faster.

- I use a map to review the extent of the Roman Empire 2000 years ago. (I make a timeline of the past 2100 years above my whiteboard for regular reference in all subjects.) Talk about how Rome fell apart and Latin became the Romance languages (show location on map): "In Italy, Latin became _____"; and so on, through Spanish, French, Portuguese. *Let your Latino children know that they can use their knowledge of Spanish to give them insights into Latin and English words.* Tell them they know a lot of Latin already by knowing Spanish and this will help them become extra-strong in English.

- Initiate The following "Body of English" Chart:

During vocabulary development, guide the children to place their words upon the Body Of English according to the words' roots — by post-its, cards, etc. Words with roots other than Greek, French, Germanic, or Latin should be posted near the feet. Vocabulary words can be assigned for research and investigation and posted upon the chart as the children discover their word origins. (Below: I got fancy with DaVinci, but I originally outlined my own body on butcher paper and labeled it with crayons.)

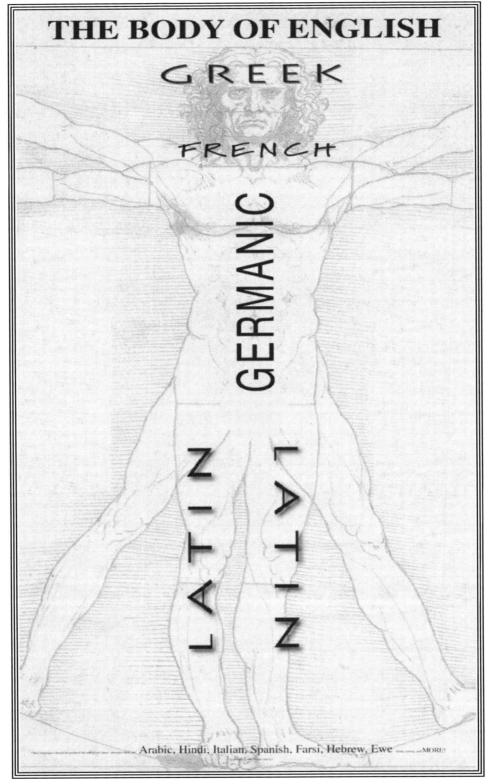

The Body of English

Writing: Show, Not Tell

At year's end, I always ask the children what was **memorable** about the year and one of the most common responses is "learning about the Dark Ages". As an adjunct lesson to the *Legend of English* lesson, I use the first part of the movie "The Dark Ages" (downloadable via iTunes or via the DVD from the History Channel) because of its iconic visuals on the recreations of the Fall of Rome and the destitution of the people afterwards. As I show this video, I pause it at several visually striking key spots and do a "**Show, Not Tell**" series of quick-write exercises, emphasizing the **power** of **sensory** descriptions. There are many good lessons on "Show, Not Tell"; simply adapt any lessons to the children you have. (My colleague Dan Anderson astutely remarked, "Education is teaching the children you have in front of you today.")

Before they write, I review our previous lesson on "**Plain, Silver, and Golden**" kinds of sentences.

I captured the the following "Show, not tell" from http://www.writedesignonline.com/assignments/shownottell.html.

Tell: The pizza was delicious.

Show: Steam rising up off the melted cheese made my mouth water. The first bite, my teeth sinking into the cheese through the tomato sauce and into the moist crust, made me chew and swallow rapidly. Even the cheese and tomato sauce, sticking to my fingertips, begged to be licked.

Tell: He is angry.

Show: Sitting at his desk, his jaw tightened. His eyes flashed heat waves at me. The words erupted from his mouth, "I want to talk to you after class." The final hiss in his voice warned me about his feelings.

Tell: The morning was beautiful.

Show: Behind the mountains, the sun peaked brightly, ready to start a new day. The blue sky remained silent yet showed signs of sadness. The wind whispered through the trees as the cheerful sun rose. The birds sang gently by my window as if they wanted to wake me up.

Create Comprehension
(Can-See-Do)

Focus Questions

1. Why did Rome want to conquer Britannia?

2. What language did the Romans speak across their empire?

3. After the Romans left, who invaded Britannia?

4. English is made up mainly from what FOUR languages?

6~12 Other questions provided by class or by the student.

Tell your students **their task is to make up a test** and they are to give their test to their parent/caretaker. Here are the rules: the questions can be in any style the student thinks (fill in the blank, multiple choice, etc.); for three questions they will create, they must select from the question stems below. Review good and poor questions. Add your own or make a test from the whole class!

Questions from the California STARs
(<u>S</u>tandardized <u>T</u>esting <u>A</u>nd <u>R</u>eporting program)

Which came first,

Where did .....

The author says _____. That meant_____.

Why were... / Why was... / Why did...

What was the reason ....

In the sentence "_____" , what does "_____" mean?

Use this pre-post-create/can-see-do comprehension model in your other reading activities. The students love making up their own tests! Everyone enjoys seeing comprehension rise.

Word Investigations

After the students bring back their tests from their parents, tell the students that the "Legend of English" just supercharged their ability to learn new words. And they can understand more about words and release hidden powers. Tell the children that some words have keys to dozens of other words — and much can be learned by investigation. Learning the history of a word or its *etymology* will now make more sense.

Tell your students that there is one good reason it is important to learn this: if they learn the word stems (*"morpheme"*, the tiniest shape of meaning) of just a few words, suddenly they can figure out hundreds or even thousands of new words.

Walk them through each line of the Word Investigation worksheet. Have the students follow you through a dictionary or dictionary.com (and, if necessary, a thesaurus, and an etymology dictionary or etymologyonline.com) and fill out a couple of sheets with them. From time to time, assign certain key words for a **complete investigation**.

I tell the children that while this seems like a boring task, they learn something deep about words and it empowers their speech and writing. I give homework passes as incentives to well-completed investigations.

As a follow up to this lesson, I engage the children for a few weeks of studying word roots.

Proto-Indo-European

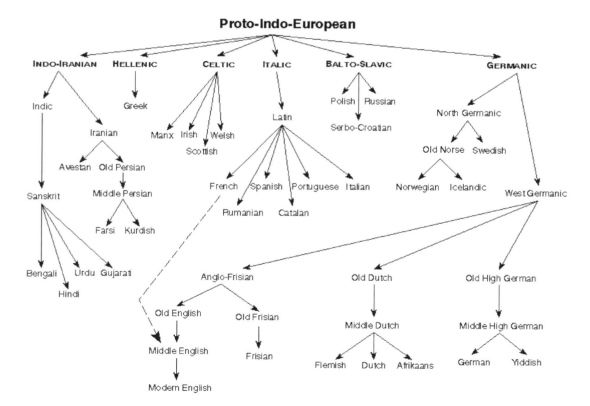

Word Investigation Chart

1) Word: _____

2) Part(s) of speech/kind of word: _____

3) vowel sounds/ pronunciation/diacritical marks: _____

4) Definitions/sentences:

_____

_____

_____

_____

_____

_____

_____

_____

5) synonyms:

_____

_____

_____

6) antonyms:

_____

_____

_____

8) Etymology: _____

Language(s): old word(s): meaning(s)

9) Affixes/morpheme: _____

10) I learned: _____

_____

As a class, practice filling out an investigation sheet on the following words: "awareness", "sensitivity", "receded", "attention". Help them record and discern pronunciation guides and etymologies. (Etymologyonline.com is my favorite.)

awareness; noun, "the state of awareness", in line with "wary"...

sensitivity

receded

attention

Tell them: "As you finish doing a word research on all the key terms, you will build your vocabulary force. You will gather amazing power, you will see."

‒‒

Autobiographical Frames

1. **Framing (and Filling) An Autobiographical Story**
2. **Autobiographical Clozing**
3. **I AM Poem**

Framing (and Filling) An Autobiographical Story

Now they take their timeline of their life, and together with the elements of story they have learned, and write about a brief autobiographical incident that made them change in some way -- because they learned a lesson. [Please note: Language Arts Programs, District assessments, and the State DOE often require something in this vein in the first weeks of school.]

Instruct the children that when they write their story they need to include *most* of the following parts (or answer most of the questions in every box). Instinctively, they want to write only the **Body** part (that is the main part after all). But I tell the children they need to put "box-ends" on the main story, a little intro and a wrap up. On the board, I draw three boxes as below and make these seven points in it. I give the boxes (as drawn below) and the 7 points within them as homework and tell them they will get a small test on it the next day.

Intro
1 paragraph
 	
1. Grabber First Sentence!
 	
2. Set-up or summary.
	The Body
	3 paragraphs
	
	3. The 7 W's
	Where (could be in Intro)
	When (could be in Intro)
	Who was there?
	Why were they important?
	
	What happened?
	What happened first?
	    after that?
	    then?
	    end?
	
	Why was it important?
		Wrap Up
		1 paragraph
		
		4. How did you feel?
		5. How did others feel and why was this important?
		6. What changed for you?
		7. How do you feel now?

Again, teach the parts in isolation, i.e., first teach and engage the features of the Intro only! Take this Introductory paragraph, and only this paragraph, through the writing process. Only when you have re-written this paragraph two or three times, do you tackle the Body. In addition to the **W**'s, **invite** them to include as many **E**'s as possible (see next page). Take the two or three paragraphs that constitute the Body through the writing process (likewise for the Wrap-Up). Breaking it up like this helps the weaker writers and clarifies the stronger ones.

You might add some "E"s

S E E E E E E ?

Examples

Events

Experiences

Explain

Evidence

Excitement

Elaboration

In the next few pages are charts and rubrics to use in your teaching.

Go through the PACES
before you turn it in!

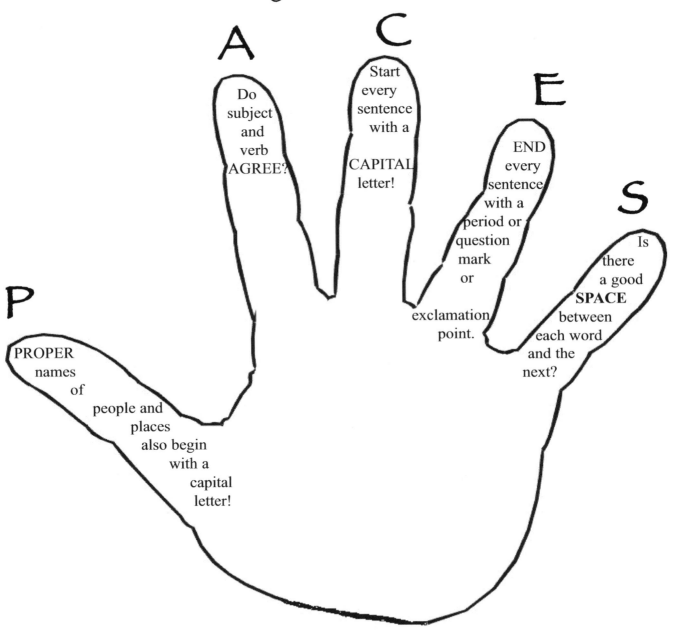

Five Finger Editing

Autobiographical Clozing

Use the following prompts to write about yourself:

1. Write two-three adjectives about yourself, and say why.

2. How old you are, and why you like being this age.

3. I know how to _____

4. I want to learn _____

5. I wish I could _____

6. When I have free time, I _____.

7. I'm happy when _____.

8. When I'm alone, I _____.

9. I cry when _____ .

10. My favorite subject in school is _____, because _____.

11. My favorite color is _____ because

12. One of the best books I've ever read is _____. I liked it because

_____.

13. I love to visit _____ because _____.

14. When I grow up, _____ .

15. I would love to visit _____, so that I _____.

Plain, Silver, Golden Sentences

1. **Plain** -- says a LITTLE clearly! Every writing needs short sentences. <u>Every communication needs some simple sayings</u>, but most plain sentences need to be enriched.

> e.g. "She had black hair."
> "He was nice."
> "We stopped."

2. **Silver** -- says MORE. Find the nouns and add adjectives, find the verbs and consider adverbs;

> e.g. "He was friendly and happy."
> "She had black, shiny hair."
> "We stopped abruptly."

3. GOLDEN -- says it ALL! Use similes, metaphors, personification, hyperbole, alliteration.

e.g. "He was so kind, his heart lighted the room."
"Her long, black hair was so fine, the sun glistened off of it in sheets of light."
"We stopped so abruptly I thought my eyeballs would pop out."

The best writings have <u>all</u> three: plain, silver and golden.

A Rubric for Checking Your Descriptive Paragraph

<u>FIX</u>   <u>YES</u>

0 1 2 - 3 4 5   Does the first sentence introduce or tell what is being described?

0 1 2 - 3 4 5   Do the other sentences tell more about what is being described? Good supporting sentences?

0 1 2 - 3 4 5   Are sentences in logical order? Does it make sense? Jump around too much?

0 1 2 - 3 4 5   Does the paragraph paint a clear and accurate picture of what is being described? Could someone else draw a picture from your description?

0 1 2 - 3 4 5   Is every sentence Capitalized?/Punctuated? Is it Neat?

0 1 2 - 3 4 5   Simple Sentences? Senses?
0 1 2 - 3 4 5   Silver Synonyms, Adjectives, Adverbs or Antonyms?
0 1 2 - 3 4 5   Golden Metaphors, Hyperbole, Simile, or Personification?
0 1 2 - 3 4 5   Are the senses evokes; are descriptive words used?

SENSES

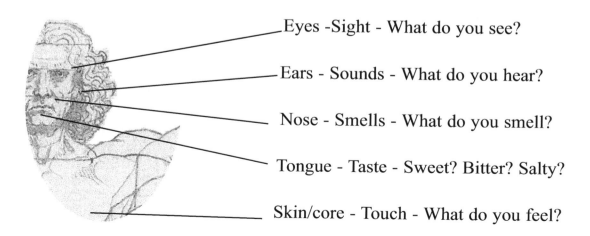

Eyes -Sight - What do you see?

Ears - Sounds - What do you hear?

Nose - Smells - What do you smell?

Tongue - Taste - Sweet? Bitter? Salty?

Skin/core - Touch - What do you feel?

I AM Poem

Have the children make an "I am" Poem using the most (or all) of the following categories. I give extra credit to those who illustrate their poems (by pictures or illustrations). I also give the children my son Salem's example (see next page) so that they have a feel for their assignment.

I AM _____ , <u>+ descriptor OR action OR why OR Feeling OR ??</u>

nice animal

color/hue

sound

weather

instrument

season

plant

water

touch

fierce animal

heart

wild weather

sound

idea/question

trouble with humans

great about humans

smell/taste

feeling

animal (flying)

color / bright

waters

idea

awe

Salem's Example

I am a Wombat asleep in its burrow.

I am the color of the evening sunlight.

I am the sound of joyful laughing.

I am the hurricane roaring.

I am the guitar laughing with fear.

I am the spring blossoming with colors.

I am the sword grass being eaten by a wombat.

I am the wild salt water washing away.

I am the light of god, the wonder we feel.

I am the electron circling around the proton.

I am the tiger chasing its prey.

I am the heart sparkling.

I am the lightning striking the Earth.

I am the sound of quietness.

I am the question: "What is everything?" "It's a mystery."

I am a nice, warm, sunny day.

I am the rainforest being cut down.

I am the summer, where people play happily.

I am the happiness filling the earth.

I am the Tazmanian tiger roaring with fear, happiness, laughter, and hunger.

I am the color of the heart.

I am the high pitched sound of drums.

I am the peregrine falcon following the wind.

I am the clear waters of Lake Leelanau.

I am the mind of all of these things.

ReTale
Retelling a Fairy Tale

Read or otherwise investigate other tellings of fairy tales. My favorite is *The Paper Bag Princess* by Robert N. Munsch, where the Princess is a stronger character than her arrogant suitor, and who prevails by standing for her own knowledge. My second favorite is "Fractured Fairy Tales by Peabody" from the Rocky and Bullwinkle Show, but there are many more.

Co-generate a list of fairy tales on the board. These should include simple stories like: Little Red Riding Hood, Goldilocks, Three Little Pigs, etc. The children are to pick a fairy tale, and quick-write a one paragraph summary or "moral of the story". Once this brief summary is done, they are free to re-write it with alternate set-ups and/or endings. My recent favorite submission was "Fairy-Tale Mix-Up" where some of my students collaborated on a story that wove its way through a series of different fairy tales and Mother Goose rhymes.

I do this activity as an **extra-credit quick-write**, where groups get to read their story and show their class their drawings. It is a great Friday afternoon activity where students get to laugh and be proud to show their works.

Below please find my daughter's story, which I read to the class as a sample. While I did provide the bare structures of the story, my second-grade daughter Ella wrote every "zinger". I said, "Once upon a time, there were three little pigs who left home...." and then paused. She would finish and perhaps go on and on. When she would "finish", I'd provide another prompt and she'd respond. This technique is easily transferred to a class, where younger kids will need more prompts, but the older kids can take the ball and run with it.

The Really Real Story of

The Three Little Pigs

by Ella and Papa MARRERO

Illustrations Borrowed off the Internet

Three Little Pigs

Here they are

Once upon a time, as you know, there were three little pigs who left home, *just like you will someday.* But what you don't know is all three pigs had the same amount of money and went to the same place to buy their building supplies.

In all the stories you've heard, the first little pig "suddenly meets a man carrying straw." No way. He didn't just poof out of nowhere.

He was standing right next to the guy selling sticks, who was standing next to the guy selling bricks.

You get the idea, it was at the market beside the fair.

What the other stories also don't tell you were the sales pitches each vendor was selling.

The first guy squawked, "Step right up my friend, set your house up easily. <u>Choose straw</u>. It's fast to build, warm to snuggle, beautiful to look at, and leaves you with a lot of money in your pocket! With the cash you will have left, you can fill it with furniture, throw a huge party and take some time off." Needless to say, the first pig was tricked, and off he went. He wanted to play and took the easy way.

The second salesman said, "Get your strong sticks here. They're easy to use and assemble — all you have to do is lay them in a row, and stand them up quickly. Stronger than straw, of course, and with the money you have left over, you could relax in the sun and have a quiet summer."

You can guess that the second pig was also tricked from his laziness.

The third vendor was the least exciting, but the most honest. He said, "Bricks cost a lot. You won't have much money left over, but you will have a nice home for a long, long time."

What would you do? Have fun and forget about you-know-who?

The third pig was glad he wasn't lazy or tricked.

Now some stories go on and on about the bad wolf huffing and puffing, but it really happened just like that. The first and second pigs lost their homes and their lives, or maybe they had to live with their wiser sibling.

In any case, the story was not about the wolf or pigs, but about making wise choices.

Author Ella Marrero laughing the night she wrote this book

Unit Three: Brief and Long-Lasting Happiness
Dynamic Writing on Wisdom

Hellenic: King Midas and the Greatest Richness

How You Feel Affects How You See

**"If you give a pig and a boy everything they want,
you get a good pig and a bad boy."**

— An 88 year old Tennessee farmer responded,
when asked what he had learned in life.

Common Core Standards Addressed

Reading Lit. 2, 9, 10

Foundation Skills. 4 a, c,

Writing Narratives 1a, c, d, 2a, c, e, 5, 9a, 10

Teacher's Introduction: Brief and Long-Lasting Happiness

The distinction between inherent happiness and the happiness that is *caused* forms a central theme in most every great religion and philosophical persuasion. It is not the things or the power you have that makes you happy, it's what you are and how you value and relate to others and creatures. It has always been noted that happiness is not in things, but in feeling, in appreciation, in being, in love. Understanding the distinction between inherent, expressive happiness and caused, acquired happiness forms the very foundation of character: Morality itself could be said to be described by this distinction. For in simply noticing this difference between true happiness and excitement, a worthier life is nourished; an unexamined life is truly not worth living. This is values education at its core.

The distinction between "High Happiness" and "Deep Happiness" provides a perfect opportunity to teach Compare-Contrast analysis and the subsequent two-point paragraph. I have done this quite successfully in grades 2-6. I begin by holding up two similar yet different objects: I use the always convenient marker and a pencil and ask students to compare and contrast them; tell me what is the same and different about the objects. As volunteers explain, I note useful sentence fragments they use. "While one is _____ , the other _____; Both are _____; etc. Of course, I also draw a Venn diagram and put the distinctive qualities in the appropriate places.

Because inherent happiness is **native** and is the simplest of all feelings, it doesn't require any form of special knowledge to feel it. Sage counsel has always pointed to a childlike (not childish!) awe in mature living. Plus, children in their **naive** state of openness can also easily feel this basic happiness. They enjoy (and come to understand in their own way) the lesson of inherent happiness' seniority over acquired glee via a plethora of stories throughout the world. In this section, the *Core Stories* begin with the idealized story of gold-loving King Midas.

As you may know, Dionysus only reluctantly gave the magic touch to King Midas for taking care of his friend Silenus, who had lost his way and fallen asleep in King Midas' rose garden. And of course, Midas, upon attaining his reward, ran around turning everything to gold, until no other enjoyments remained, not even the natural pleasure of eating, drinking, and smelling the roses. Most poignant of all, he lost his relationship with his daughter. Gold without relationship was the horror foretold in Dionysus' reluctance.

When Midas realized that he had wished for a tragedy, he was truly sorry for the real treasure he had lost. On the basis of this turning from acquiring happiness in objects to relational, harmonious appreciation, he washed everything in water from a nearby river, restoring every thing and everyone to their greater-than-gold natural state. Realizing that happiness was not found in things but in participating in the open wonder of relational existence itself, King Midas left his kingdom and went with his daughter to live in a small cabin near a meadow in the woods. This most foundational of all lessons guides us to locate true happiness. Children love writing about this preference for real happiness. Again I quote my friend and fellow Dan Alderson, "Great ideas inspire great writing."

This primary feeling at one's core coincides with the deepening of character. This core-happiness, not to be confused with gleefulness or even a "positive outlook", comprises the deep substance of an intelligent life. Happiness distinct from excitement widens the door to deep, full character. And while we cannot walk our children through that door, we can help them clarify their choosing. The stories and writing assignments in this section, combined with our own growth, sensitivity, and confession, guide our children to feel this primary urge to true happiness, and also confirms in them their own emotional durability. They strengthen their ability to feel toward long-lasting happiness in every situation, even in the midst of difficult circumstances. This preference for native, relational happiness is the foundational wise choice of all other wise choices.

A corollary theme immediately appears: **how we feel affects how we see**. As we notice happiness and unhappiness and a vast range of emotions, we also notice how our perception of our world is colored by how we feel. We see poorly when we are unhappy and lazy; we see better when we are excited or energetic; we see best when we are happy and engaged. Wisdom about perception itself naturally arises when we give our attention to this primary issue of "true" and lasting happiness.

It is good and essential to talk about happiness directly, learn about happiness with your children, and demonstrate happiness to them. Let them simply know that happiness does not come from things but is always at one's core, and **is magnified** in caring relations. (Not in "getting" but by giving.) True happiness is not acquired but shared; not earned, but felt. Such straightforward attention to this most essential need provides an inviting avenue to the unthreatened, simple feeling of natural joy. Let us share this openness with our children and teach them to share it in ordinary and intelligent ways with the world.

Find Synonyms for *The Story of King Midas*
(Remember: *Thesaurus* is Latin for *"Treasure"*.)

inevitable _____

luxurious _____

abundant _____

recognizing _____

elated _____

fragrance _____

disappointment _____

statue _____

liveliness _____

vibrance _____

wise _____

Hellenic: King Midas and the Greatest Richness

The Story of King Midas is a classic Hellenic myth on the tragedy that is inevitable when true happiness is not noticed. It partially refers to the King of Lydia, in his gold-rich Pactulus river valley in southwest Asia Minor.

Midas was once a very rich king who ruled the land of Phygia. He had everything a king could want. He lived in a huge castle surrounded by rose gardens and all kinds of beautiful and luxurious things. He had all the good food he could eat, and shared his abundant life with his wonderful daughter, Zoe (meaning "Life").

But Midas thought that his huge pile of gold made him happiest of all. Every day, he would begin to count his gold until he became so excited that he would laugh and laugh and throw the gold up in the air to shower himself with his gold coins. Sometimes he would even lie down and cover himself with golden things, giggle and giggle, and roll around in it like a baby.

Dionysus, the god of celebration, went travelling through Midas' kingdom. Dionysus had a friend named Silenus who wandered away from his travelling party and fell asleep in Midas' famous rose garden. Midas, upon recognizing Silenus, took special care of him for eleven days and then returned him safely back to Dionysus. The god, delighted and grateful to see Silenus, said to King Midas, "You have done a great service by taking care of my friend for me that I want to grant you any wish your heart desires."

In an instant Midas replied, "I wish that everything that I touch would turn to gold!"

Dionysus frowned, "Are you sure that's what you want?"

"Oh yes," Midas answered, "gold makes me completely happy!"

"Very well," Dionysus sighed reluctantly, "starting tomorrow morning, everything you touch will turn into gold."

The next morning Midas woke up and couldn't wait to try out his golden touch. Before he got out of bed, he reached over and touched his bedside table and instantly it turned to gold, just as Dionysus had promised. Midas had the golden touch!

"It works, it works!!!" he shouted as he sprang out of bed. He touched the chair, the table, the rug, the door, the fireplace, his bathtub, a picture, and went running like a madman on and on through his palace, touching one thing after another until he was out of breath and hungry, but still elated.

Midas felt all bubbly as he entered his dining hall. He sat down at the breakfast table, leaned over and pulled a rose close to his nose to enjoy its fragrance. But when he touched the flower, its sweet smell poured forth no more. It was now cold metal. "I'll have to sniff them without touching them from now on!" he thought to himself with disappointment.

Without thinking, he popped a grape into his mouth, but he nearly broke a tooth for the grape had also turned to gold. Very carefully, he tried to eat a muffin, but his teeth only clanked on the now hard bread, once so soft and delicious. "Gold again," thought Midas. "Oh no! Everything I touch turns to gold. Perhaps…" he said, as he grabbed his wine glass to take a drink, but immediately he began to cough and choke as liquid gold slid down his throat.

Fear suddenly gobbled his joy. At that moment his favorite cat jumped up into his lap, wanting to get stroked and petted, but was instantly turned into a metal statue. Instead of snuggling his fingers into warm purring fur, Midas' fingers touched only hardness and coldness. He started to cry. "Am I only to feel gold's coldness for the rest of my life?" he shouted through his tears.

Zoe, hearing her father cry, ran over to comfort him with a hug. He tried to stop her, but accidently touched her. Instantly before him was only a gold statue of what before had been his joyous daughter. Midas cried and cried.

Finally, he held his arms up and pleaded, "Oh Dionysus, gold is not what I really want after all! I already had all I wanted all along. I just want to be able to hug my daughter again, to hear her laugh, to see her smile, to touch and smell my roses and pet my cat and share food with my loved ones. Please help me, save me from this golden curse."

Dionysus, being a very kind god, whispered an answer into Midas' heart. "You may undo your golden touch and restore those golden statues to life again, but it will cost you all the gold in your kingdom."

"Anything," Midas cried, "I want life, not gold."

"Ahh! You have made the wise choice of the heart. Then go to the river Pactulus and wash your hands at its source. Carry the water back home in jugs and pour it over everything that you've changed to gold. That water, along with your changed heart, will restore the liveliness to those things that your greed froze into metal."

Midas ran to the river and washed his hands, grateful to Dionysus for another chance. He watched in wonder as the gold flowed from his hands into the sand at the bottom of the riverbed. Quickly he filled a jug with water and hurried to his royal palace to pour it over his daughter. He wetted his hand from the jug and petted the cat.

In an instant, the empty silence reawakened into laughter and the music of Zoe's voice and his cat purring. The sounds filled the rooms and hall of the palace once again. Midas and his daughter hugged and laughed over and over again. Then she helped him bring jugs of Pactulus water back to the palace to pour over every last twig, rose, rock, rug, bed, bread, and grape that still gleamed gold.

Midas rejoiced as the vibrance of life returned to his garden, palace, and heart. He now wisely loved the Brightness of life instead of the luster of gold. To celebrate, he gave away the rest of his money and possessions and moved to a cabin on the edge of the forest. There they enjoyed the simple pleasures of life with each other as the greatest treasure of all.

*****

Simple Assessment for King Midas

Name:_____ Date:_____

1) a. Name three characters in the story.

    b. Sensually describe the setting (sights? smells? sounds? activity?)

2) What genre is this story?.

3) In the beginning of the story, what did Midas think made him happy?

    What terrible events followed that desire?

4) In the middle of the story, what did Midas want?

    How did his want change?

    What events followed that desire?

6) Why did someone make up this story?

Teacher Follow-up

Discussion: 1st Accentuate the Distinction

Ask: Was King Midas really happy when he could turn things into gold?   OR

Was he really happy when he got his daughter back?

Sharpen the distinction:

"Did he think he was happy when he first got the golden touch? Was it long-lasting happiness?

"Was he sure he was happy when he got his daughter back? Did that happiness go away?"

With this kind of accentuation, explain to your child in your own words how the happiness of relationship and sharing is greater than the happiness of things and possessions. Using the supplemental stories, guide them to feel the difference between brief and long-lasting happiness. Develop simple terms such as passing enjoyments and long-lasting happiness; excited <--> truly happy; 'high happy' <--> 'deep happy' (more below).

Remember to let them feel good about excitement and pleasure; and feel better about empathy & love. The nascent mind tends to see only black and white: as if brief happiness is bad, and only long-lasting happiness is good. Guide them to feel both freely and intelligently. But also emphasize: IF you have to make a choice between high happy and deep happy, it is wise to choose depth. Blend this theme into the frustrations of ordinary events.

Ask:

"Can you feel excited and not happy? ... Like just eating a sweet for sad consolation.

"Can you feel excited and happy at the same time? ... Like getting something from someone you love.

"Is excitement like happiness?

"Which is best, stimulation or love?

"Can you feel happy without excitement? ... Just sitting and doing nothing and still feeling deeply happy?

"Is half a piece of cake better than none at all?

"Can you feel joy and thirst at the same time?

"Can you eat something tasty and still be unhappy?

"Can you be happy even if *you can't always get what you want*? " (**Can** you, not **would** you! ...And yes, play the Rolling Stones song for them, if you want.)

More Discussion Prompts:

- the Latin word for "heart" is "core". (Core <-> superficial, "inside" <-> "outside", etc.)
- "Core" is the root of courage, as well as encourage.
- Would you rather have a dollar now or a nickel a day forever?
- (For the older students), invite them to reflect upon the following proposition of Socrates and how this might relate to this "core" consideration:

"Shallow men and women live

that they may eat and drink,

whereas happy men and women eat and drink

that they may live."

-- Sokrates of Athens, 469-399 B.C.E.

A Bit of Sweet Theatre

A Venn Diagram in Preparation to Write

I like to break my rule of no-sugar and begin the lesson by dramatically opening a large bag of Hersey's kisses. (I use the gold ones with the almond inside.)

Announce the rules as you place one on every desk. No touching!

They may lose the kiss if they touch it or don't pay attention; everyone will eat their kiss together with everyone else at the end of the lesson.

As you pass them out, **ask** the children what the (gold) kisses remind them of? — King Midas' gold of course.

Ask the children if gold makes you happy?

Ask if candy makes you truly happy? Truly happy? As happy as having a friend?

As you conduct your discussion and lesson, reward attention and participation with an extra candy every now and then. The game-like quality helps keep them involved.

Return to the whiteboard and draw a LARGE Venn diagram and write Happy on one side and Excited on the other. Challenge your children with 10-15 minutes of discussion and guidance co-generating a list of the differences and similarities between deep happy and high happy (or between true happiness and excitement).

Referring to your Venn Diagram on the board, ask: Was Midas happy or was he excited when he could turn things to gold by his touch? He thought he was happy. When he got his daughter back was he truly happy? Did he think so or was he sure? Indicate these differences/examples on the board. Have them copy your co-created Venn diagram. At last, everyone, **in unison,** eats their kiss as an example of "deep and excited happiness together".

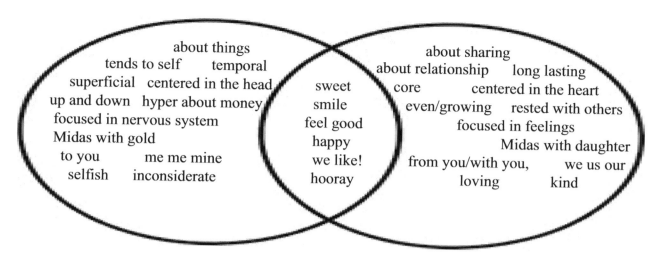

Make sure everyone copies the **Venn diagram** from the board. (They will need it for homework.) Now ask students to give an example in their own life when they were excited-happy. Follow this with class examples of being deeply-happy. Or both, or just simply happy without excitement, etc. "Ever remember a time when you were happy for no reason at all? Quiet and happy?" Generate a discussion of other stories using this theme of true vs false happiness. (Christmas Carol, The Pearl, etc.) Did King Midas (Scrooge, etc) think they were happy when they got their "gold"? Was Midas (Scrooge, etc) sure they were truly happy when relationship was restored to the center of their life?

Please note: Guide the children away from black & white judgments—e.g. that excitement is 'bad' and happiness is 'good'— and help them to realistically value all forms of 'good' feeling.

Let them feel that they can develop a kind of relationship with physical things, like an instrument; and deep happiness can come from such artful development with some 'things'. This relational development of an art is quite different than collecting things and the latest toy to simulate the sensation of happiness.

By creating a continuum, we do not fall into the myopia of success and failure, "good" or "bad", but rather encourage acceptance, understanding, and growth. By showing a continuum rather than either/or dyads, we help them see that there are many kinds of "good feeling" but deep happiness is simply the best.

Writing a Compare-Contrast Paragraph

Begin with this Pre-Write: Use the following pre-write to assist your students with the basic structure of how to write a simple 2-point paragraph. (Modify the sentence forms according to the the students' abilities.) As a class, quickly co-create a simple example, perhaps using the differences and the sameness of a pencil and a marker.

───────────── • **THE TWO-POINT PARAGRAPH** • ─────────────

The two points/things/ideas I want to talk about are

_____ & _____ .

Thing "A" is _____ .

and I think/ it is important because _____ .

Thing "B" is _____ and I think/ it is important because _____

_____ .

Idea A is similar to idea B _____ . (repeat?)

Idea B is similar to idea A _____ . (repeat?)

Point A is different from to B _____ and also

_____ .

Both A and B_____ .

_____ .

A _____ , but B _____ .

Concluding remarks: _____

_____

With the demonstration concluded, have them write (for homework): Take their Venn diagram they copied from the board and write two paragraphs on the two kinds of happiness, with at least 5 sentences each. Tell them to be sure to leave a space between each line, or use "double-space" if word processing. Tell them that this will be the beginning of a three week process where they will work on one small piece of writing and re-writing.

Before the students can turn-in their work, I introduce/reteach editorial marks. (We regularly practice "fix it" sentences such as Daily Oral Language.) Using a digital camera and projector, I guide the students on how to make editorial marks and discuss **why.** (First we do the Daily Oral Language "fix-its", then student volunteered papers. This is an example of teaching effectiveness empowered by a simple technology.)

Once I am confident that a basic understanding of editorial marks is established, I require the children to "editorialize" their own paper, seeing how many improvements they can make. Have the children tally how many editorial improvements they made and give themselves a point for every mark they make on their own paper.

Next, incorporate "peer editing" into this process, where everyone gets points for making correct editorial improvements to someone else's paper, writing in a different colors. (Author's marks writing in pencil, first editor is in red, second editor in blue.) I use a collaborative online working environment, but I find that exchanging papers works best for marking and excitement.

Guess what? For homework, they must rewrite! the paper again, incorporating as many of the marks that they agree with. I then collect the papers, and ask for volunteer papers to editorialize through the digital camera as time allows. Later, I make a round of my own marks for the rest.

As soon as I can, I hand the papers back and ask the students to look over their papers to make sure they understand each editorial stroke and comment. Then, they are in for a another re-write, incorporating all the editorializing. I find that I must require my students to cross off each editorial mark to "prove" they saw it and used it. Otherwise, they miss lots!

As a responsive teacher, I notice common errors (e.g. quotation markings, commas) and give mini-lessons on these grammatical points and use a variety of methods to reteach, instruct and practice.

When they think they are done, I add another addition: I have everyone get out their most finished work, and they must circulate them to other students. For 10 minutes we exchange papers 10 times, pausing for one minute every "Pass!". The students are to read the other paper and take notes from what others have said that they liked, writing down ideas for saying something in their own way, OR repeating something others have said (with attribution, "Like Aleysha said...").

Then I tell them to rewrite their paper yet again, and while they will be including as much of the community notes as possible, they also include the other quotes or examples that have been discussed in class for the last ~two weeks. Because during this editorializing-enlarging phase of their writing piece, you will be also engaging and analyzing the other Core Stories in a other ways. In class we read the short *Core Story* from China: *Hedgehog's Changing Sight,* and discuss how feeling affects perception, followed by a quickwrite.

The students also read or hear the rest of the *Core Stories* from around the world. These world stories each have something said very well and a variety of comparisons can be made between the many tongues/cultures. New pithy understandings can also be added to their notes for a final rewrite. After this, I usually tell them that they're done, but come back, if necessary, with a "couple of things I missed before."

Class Publication

I always publish these two-point, compare/contrast mini-essays in two ways: **one**, I make a hallway bulletin board; and **two**, I assemble them all into an anthology, *On Happiness*, which is sent to every home just before the holidays. Timing.

Samples of my (5th grade) students' work in this lesson:

The Two Kinds of Happiness by Nick

I want to talk abut two things: high happy and deep happiness. Deep happiness is like friends and family. High happy is like when you eat a ice cream; you like it, but it's gone in minutes.

I will give you some examples of both. Deep happiness is a feeling that lasts a long time... like being around your family and your friends. Then high happiness is money, food, and things. But what you need is love. Would you want money or not to be hugged again? You would feel terrible.

So not all the money in the world can beat love. So it's not like a new piece of jewelry. If you can buy it, it is not really happiness. It is like a story I am reading in class. All his life this guy was receiving happiness and now he is unhappy all the time. So you can't buy or receive happiness all the time, but you can give it anytime.

Compare/Contrast Assignment by Sierra

I would like to tell about High Happy and Deep Happy. They are very similar in ways ... let me explain. High -Happy is something that you have and use it once or for a while and then after you use it, its happiness gone. Example: I ate my ice-cream today, but once that the cone was eaten it was gone. Deep Happy it is just like High Happy, but lasts longer! Example: I saw my dad yesterday and when I had to leave he gave me a huge hug, I can still feel the happiness of that same huge hug.

So you see there are two ways to discuss happiness. Change the world: ask people what kind of happiness they are talking about. There are ways that you can discuss High Happiness and Deep- Happiness. First, I will say that Deep Happy is something that you can feel in your heart and will stay there forever. High Happy is when you get a toy and you play with it and once you grow out of it, it's gone. If you have fun by High Happy it's OK, but you should really be happy from Deep Happy, It lasts forever. So as you see there are two kinds of happiness, but I'm not quite done. You can be happy in many ways, but please I beg you to please appreciate Deep Happy.

The Two Kinds of Happy by D. Sanchez

There is high happy and deep happy. High happy is like winning the lottery, deep happy is like sharing the lottery with your family. Deep happiness is better than high happy because if you are high happy then you become selfish and only want things for yourself. You are deep happy when you want to share with people and you will feel happier. Deep happy is about a lot of love, and high happy is like for your self and little else. Deep happy is from the heart. High happy you can hurt someone's feelings by being selfish. When I get a present, I am high happy, when I say, "thank you," I am deep happy. High happy doesn't last forever, and deep happy last for a very long time.

High Happy and Deep Happy by Sergio

High Happy and Deep Happy are types of happiness. High Happy comes to you but only lasts a short time. For example when you get ice-cream you love it but when it's all gone you don't love anymore. Deep Happy is in your heart and it does not come and it lasts for a long time. High Happy last for a couple of minutes but Deep happy last for your lifetime. For example, you love your mom but when you get in a fight with her you mad at her, you still love her no-matter what. High Happy is similar to Deep Happy and Deep Happy is similar to High Happy. High Happy is cool, Deep Happy is great. With High Happy you think you like it but with Deep Happy you know you love it. If you think you love it, that's High Happy, and if you know you love, that's Deep Happy. It's important to realize the difference, like the Beatles said, "You can't buy love."

How You Feel Affects How You See

- Begin by talking about "Perception--How you see" by showing them the *Visual Illusions* on the next page. Guide them to see the Visuals here (many more if you "Google" *Visual Illusions*).

- **Read** aloud or **tell** them the following stories:"Pandas in Paradise" and "Hedgehog's Changing Sight". Have a discussion about how perception changes according to your emotions.

- Reiterate **how we feel affects how we see**. As we notice happiness and unhappiness and a vast range of emotions, we also notice how our perception of our world is colored by how we feel. *We see poorly when we are unhappy and lazy; we see better when we are excited or energetic; we see best when we are happy and engaged.* (Therefore, it is *important* to feel towards happiness.)

- Ask for volunteers who can attest to "seeing" this change. A few volunteer stories out loud as a prewrite for this quickwrite stimulates the whole class. If they can't think of a time for themselves personally, have them reflect on a story such as "A Christmas Carole" and write about how Scrooge's perception of Christmas changed.

- **Challenge** your students to weave this point about feeling and perception into the characters' description.

Visual Illusions

Two Faces or Wineglass?

Young or Old Woman?

The Center Circles Below are the Same Size!

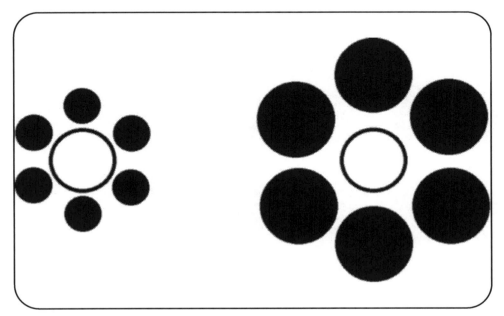

Asian: Pandas in Paradise

There is a story amongst the pandas, that, after death, all the pandas who had been selfish all their lives go to the land of Torment. In the land of Torment, there is a huge table, with a large pot of delicious rice in the center. Around the table are chopsticks to reach the rice, but the table is so large that the chopsticks are very, very long. All the pandas sit around the table, pick up a bite of rice, but, because the chopsticks are longer than their arms, they cannot put the rice in their mouths. The pandas spill and grunt and cry and complain all the time.

But the happy pandas who had learned to share go to Paradise after their life. In the land of Paradise, just like in the land of Torment, there is a huge table, with a large pot of rice in the center. And just like the land of Torment, around the table are very, very long chopsticks to reach the rice. But in Paradise, all the pandas sit around the table, pick up a bite of rice, and feed a friend. Then a friend feeds them back. They laugh and celebrate all the time.

*****

Asian: The Hedgehog's Changing Sight

I elaborated upon this classic Chinese story to re-emphasize the corollary
about growing happiness: your perception changes according to how you feel
— and when you are happy, your perception is most real.

A hedgehog lost his favorite digging spade and was very unhappy. He suspected the bigger hedgehog who lived next door had stolen it. His neighbor looked like he stole it, he acted like he stole it, he sounded like he stole it, he even smelled

like he stole it. He was afraid his neighbor would steal something else.

But then the hedgehog found his spade. Suddenly his neighbor didn't look like he stole it, didn't act like he stole it, didn't sound like he stole it, he even smelled nice again.

This change puzzled hedgehog. He told his story to Panda. Panda said "Yes, I have learned that how I feel affects how I see and think. If I am hungry, bamboo looks like food; if I am full, I see its beauty."

Hedgehog told his story and the story of the panda to the old farmer. The farmer said, "Yes, I have learned to be grateful for what I do have, it's no sense being unhappy for what I do not have. If I only have millet left to eat I am not sad, but glad to have something to eat. And if it is harvest, and bounty surrounds me, I am grateful to have something to eat. And so my world is always full."

Hedgehog told his story, the panda's story and the farmer's story to a travelling musician. The musician jumped with glee and began to sing,

"Don't put everything down,
just so you can feel big,
it is the world that is big,
it is the life that is grand;

Let us love and not hate;
whatever we have and
whatever we see,
let our eyes delight the world,
let us always truly see.

let our eyes delight the world,
let me carry you home;
we can be always free,
and sing happily;
let us always truly see,
let us always be happy."

Hedgehog clapped and clapped and clapped. The musician scooped up the hedgehog, skipped and sang all the way to hedgehog's house. Hedgehog was very, very happy and his neighbor looked like a very good friend.

*****

Unit Four: Self-Knowledge
Children Compose Simple Self-Understanding

Primary Theatre: Narcissus at the Pond

Hand Squeeze

"A Time I Was Selfish"

Daedalus or Icarus?

Common Core Standards Addressed

<u>Reading Lit. 2, 9, 10</u>

<u>Writing</u> **1a, c, 2b, c, d, 3a, b, c, d, e**

Teacher's Introduction: The Two Arms of Self-Knowledge

We often think that self-knowledge is not for children, that only adults are involved in such weighty matters. We tend to forget that every tragic drama, every lesson of the fairy tale, and every moral to the story is a call to self-knowledge and useful wisdom. Let us remember that this self-awareness is an integral part of every stage and every transition. Let us explicitly cultivate self-knowledge, self-reflection, and self-awareness as the foundation to a very strong life, at every stage.

These core stories and lessons specifically address this issue of self-knowledge in two forms, what could be called "negative" and "positive". The "negative" form of self-knowledge finds selfishness, self-absorption, Narcissism, and misfortune; in the 'positive' form of self-knowledge we find true heroes as well as our own truth, and thus can live more authentically. On the "negative" side is tragedy, the tragic fate of self-fascination and confinement to self. On the 'positive' side is the good fortune of happy actions and the happiness of relatedness and authenticity. On one hand we recognize the prison of ego-centricity, on the other, our truer and wider self freely participates in a full life.

We need to know ourselves. It broadens and deepens us to understand our familial, cultural, national, and world history. And personally, within, we need to know ourselves. The voice that happily says, "I am", has tapped into empowerment and confidence; the voice that over-proudly says anything has been briefly captured by the dark side of the same force. We need to understand the negatives of self as much as we need to connect with our truth. These are the two arms of self-knowledge.

These core stories and lessons gather great strength from both sides of self-knowledge; observations of selfishness and awareness of the authentic voice. The brightness of authenticity is grounded by a sober appreciation of our darker tendency to self-orientation. To only emphasize the light of "self-esteem" is to rob our children of the night.

Parents, elders, and teachers are already naturally involved in positive forms of self-knowledge and empowerment, such as praise, rewards, and encouragement. Continue these wholeheartedly! Teachers and parents, however, do not tend to sufficiently illuminate the other half of self-knowledge, the 'negative' side of self development, pointing out selfishness and negative self-absorption. If we encourage self-empowerment and point out selfishness, we make our self-knowledge whole. This section gives parents and teacher tools to guide children into relaxed self-inspection.

It is important to remember that it is nearly impossible to do these lessons "wrong"; just to begin to discuss these important issues serves the issue itself. Our only mistake is failing to try. For in trying, we incarnate care, and if we care, we will do these lessons beautifully.

The ancient Greek myth of Narcissus contains an archetypal understanding: unhappiness is tragically linked to exclusive attention on oneself, divorced from relationship, tending toward separative and isolated habits. When we are unhappy, we tend to be selfish and re-create aspects of the myth of Narcissus. This connection between unhappiness and the avoidance of relationship is something children can learn about through images like Narcissus. In the arena of self-knowledge, we must be diligent not to discount ourselves, but rather use images and understanding to lift our attention up to others.

Overview for Narcissus

1. **Introduce** the idea of selfishness as a phenomenon that everyone experiences: you want extra dessert before others, you don't want to share something at a time you should have, etc. Ask your students if anyone can volunteer a story about a time they were selfish. Receive the story in all graciousness, but in the end, go over to the student, and announce to the rest of the class that this student was really a strong person for confessing what s/he did. Point out that it feels like you are weak when you talk about a time you were selfish, but you have to be strong to admit it. Often one of the "less cool" people are the ones who volunteer such an admission and I thoroughly enjoy praising their strength to the rest of the class.

2. **Tell** them you are going to teach them all how to be especially strong in this way and they will be learning the story of Narcissus and there will be a small theatre.

3. **Review** or complete the vocabulary for Narcissus. I always tell the kids that the word "**hubris**" is a college word for "vain" or "over-proud" or (the current lingo is "they think they're 'all that'". I challenge all the kids to use either "hubris" or "hubristic" at home and if they do so, they write up one paragraph describing how they used it, with whom, and for a completed assignment, I give them a homework pass. I let the children know that there are a few words that lets others know that you're "educated" (and you deserve the job!)

4. Do a **read aloud**, in the style of your choice and students. As the children encounter the vocabulary in the story and discussion, ask again what the meaning is.

5. Engage in the **Theatre** of "Narcissus at the Pond".

6. **Discuss** the Lessons of the Theatre.

7. **Writing** Assignment.

Vocabulary Preparation for Narcissus

nymphs _____

curse _____

rustle _____

maiden _____

mutual _____

wither _____

reflection _____

hubris _____

vain _____

myopia _____

Hellenic: Narcissus

Narcissus is the classic archetype depicting self-fascination and self-absorption.

Narcissus, son of the river-god Cephissus, was so extraordinarily beautiful that from the moment he was born, everyone who saw him fell in love with him. Narcissus thought he didn't care if others loved him and didn't think to return the love he was given. He would pass the lovely nymphs that dwelled in his father's rivers without even a glance or "hello," even though the nymphs all loved him. When everything didn't go his way, he got mad and even left home. He acted like he didn't care.

Echo, who was the fairest of the nymphs, also fell in love with Narcissus. Once she had angered the powerful goddess Hera, who then put a curse on Echo so that she could only speak what was spoken to her. Echo wanted to tell Narcissus how much she loved him, but since she couldn't, she followed him everywhere, hiding behind trees and bushes waiting for the chance to speak to him. Then, one day, she had her chance. Narcissus was separated from a group of his friends while playing in the woods when he heard a rustle of some branches. He yelled, "Who's here?"

"Here," she called.

"Then come" said Narcissus.

"Come," she cried.

"Leave your hiding place," said Narcissus, "and we'll play."

"We'll play," she called, leaping happily from behind the tree. She ran to give Narcissus a hug, but he had forgotten how to love and pushed her away. He shouted, "Take you hands off me! I hate hugs and would rather die than let you touch me."

"Touch me," Echo cried after him and continued to secretly follow Narcissus.

One day, Narcissus broke the heart of yet another maiden who prayed to the goddess Nemesis, "If he ever loves anyone, deny him what he loves, just as he has denied everyone else his love!"

Nemesis granted her the prayer. Narcissus soon came to a clear and beautiful pond. He looked down into the water, saw a fascinating face, and was instantly captured.

At first Narcissus thought it was a beautiful water spirit and fell in love. He observed from the look in the beautiful creature's eyes that the feeling was mutual. He reached to touch his beloved but the moment his hand touched the water, the reflection scattered the image and disappeared. As soon as his image in the water returned he called out, "Why do you run away? I love you."

Echo, who was hiding nearby, replied, "I love you." But Narcissus did not look up, and continued to gaze into his pond as his image reappeared.

Narcissus forgot to eat and began to wither away from loving someone who could not love him in return. Echo continued to stay near him. She kept loving him even though Narcissus was too busy loving himself to even notice. He never left the pond for the rest of his life. At the last moment, just before he died, he called to his reflection, "Farewell, I love you."

"Farewell, I love you," Echo cried.

When the nymphs and maidens who had always loved him, gathered around to honor his body with a burial, all they found in his place was a flower looking down, which they named after him.

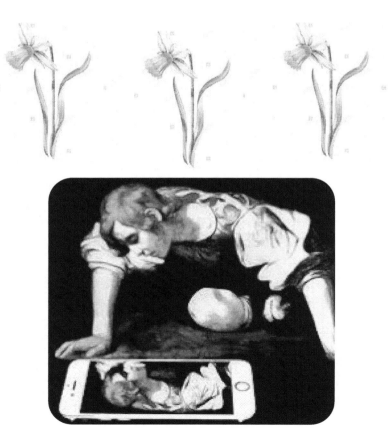

Primary Theatre: Narcissus at the Pond

This follow-up activity gently personalizes the awareness of selfishness by introducing students to the archetype of Narcissus. After the students learn the story of Narcissus, they engage in role play about what it is like to be Narcissus (unhappy, self-absorbed). Through role play students learn:

—to recognize their own choice to be Narcissus and how to look up from the pond of self-exclusiveness

—to recognize when others become Narcissus and how to help draw others out of their separateness into a state of happy relatedness.

—to recognize the difference between happy self and unhappy narcissus.

Procedure

As you engage the story of Narcissus to the children emphasize three points.
1) Did Narcissus know he was looking at himself?
2) Narcissus thought only of himself, he was completely selfish.
3) Everybody is a little like Narcissus sometimes—in some ways—right?

Role Play: Narcissus at the Pond

The purpose of this activity is to give students the opportunity to dramatize being like Narcissus (unhappy and unrelational) and becoming happy and open again. It also provides an all important lesson in giving help to another. What follows is a script of how the lesson might go. Teachers should feel free to personalize the lesson in order to make it as meaningful as possible for their students.

Let's play a game: Imagine what it felt like to be Narcissus.
Well if I'm being like this (pout and look unhappy), *am I giving love and energy to my friends and family or am I giving attention to myself?*

Invite response, then lead your children to each duplicate your example.
Let's all be Narcissus.
Pause and encourage everyone to put on an unhappy face.
Everyone is Narcissus sometimes, right?

Affirm their understanding.

Which is most like Narcissus, an open hand or a fist?
Bodily **demonstrate** with your hand.

Think of a time when you were Narcissus, a time you were a little selfish for a minute or two.
[Dramatically squeeze your hand.] *Think about what happened and what you were feeling. Were you smiling, feeling free and happy? Or were you more crunching in your feeling, worrying and maybe afraid, or frustrated and angry?*

But when you are sad or mad or unhappy, do you always want to receive the help that someone else offers you? Sometimes you just keep on being like Narcissus, and whine and collapse like this (illustrate), *or sometimes Narcissus might pretend not to hear, like this* (again illustrate), *but most of the time he'll just pout and push the help away* (illustrate and invite concurrence and other examples). *But if we keep on caring for Narcissus, I think we can get him to look up and be with us.*

When you were like Narcissus, what helped you remember to be happy and be with others again?
Record on the white board your student responses.

How can you help someone stop being Narcissus?
Invite student response. You might suggest examples like these and write them on the board:

"Clues to look up from the pond"

Invitation to relationship — "Want to play with us?

Touch of some kind to penetrate Narcissus' armor —a hug, a pat on the back, even the 'high five', 'gimme some skin'

Roughing the water (in the following Narcissus at the Pond Game) so that Narcissus cannot see his reflection — pointing out the unreality of Narcissus' appearance as his reflection disappears.

Helping them see what they are doing — "Hey, you're just being Narcissus."

Tricking Narcissus into looking up — saying something funny, joking to make them laugh.

Actively offering relationship and empathy — "You look like you're feeling unhappy. Can I help? It's OK, I like you, come out and play with me if you want."

Any combination of these.

Well, before we play the Narcissus at the Pond game, I want everyone to play a quick activity.

Hand Squeeze

The primary purpose of this game is to show how we are all mechanisms of our previous adaptation and habit formation. If we have been feeling unhappy for a long time, it may take a little time to practice feeling happy again. If we have been playing the role of Narcissus for a long time, it may at first be hard to look up or open up. In this game the adult should participate fully with the children, so that they can follow the adult's lead. **The open versus closed hand shows the primary understanding of the lesson on choosing openness over self-possession.** To effectively bridge the lessons about Narcissus with the present lessons, ask the children:

Athena gets it.

Is Narcissus [make an unhappy face] *more like this* [close one hand into a fist] *or like this* [open the hand, relax the face]?"

Everyone make a fist, like Narcissus. Now squeeze your fist hard—Narcissus is sad, he feels that no one loves him. Squeeze harder—Narcissus is mad. Whatever you do, don't stop squeezing, squeeze hard and harder! Narcissus is scared. Make the tightest fist you can and hold for as long as you can. Squeeze and squeeze and squeeze and pout and squeeze. Come on, just ten more seconds. 10, 9—squeeze—8, 7, 6, 5—squeeze, a little bit more, squeeze—4, 3, 2, 1.

Okay, now everybody gently try to open and close both of your hands. Notice the difference? The hand that has been a fist doesn't want to open easily . . or it feels funny. It is a hard or weird feeling to just open up sometimes, especially if you have had a lot of energy in being closed. And it is just that way when we are being like Narcissus. If we have been unhappy for a while, it can be difficult to be open and happy again. But it feels better to be open again, doesn't it? Just like it is better to be happy than all crunched up. Want to do it again? Okay, let's do the other hand.

The image of the closed hand and the open hand is a symbol you can use effectively again and again, in other games as well as at random. You can ask them if they would rather be "like this" (making a fist) or "like this" (making an open hand) when making a point about the superiority of happy, relational actions over unhappy, self-involved behavior. It is an image easily understood. (We revisit this image later in "The Juxtaposed Stories of the Twin Sisters, Daimonia and Destiny".)

An elaboration of this activity is to have everyone make a fist and at the same time, feign unhappiness, make an unhappy face. Then slowly open the hand and open the face and open your feeling. Even small children can understand this distinction.

Star knows the difference.

Narcissus at the Pond (cont.)

Bring out a pan or bowl of water. This will be Narcissus' pond.

Begin by **modeling** the actions of Narcissus for the entire class. Put on your best unhappy face. Ask your students if that is what you look like when you are unhappy. Do different versions of unhappiness, including self-absorption, saying to your own reflection, "Oh my, you are so good looking/smart/fascinating/cool." (Then laugh at yourself. Modeling is powerful.)

At this time you may want to re-visit with your students the worksheet of "Clues" that will help them to know how to get Narcissus to look up from the pond. The clues are the different strategies the students can use to help someone stop being Narcissus.

When the modeling and review of Clues is accomplished, announce the Game, "Narcissus at the Pond."

Teacher Prompt:

"Now let's play Narcissus. Here is the pond. Let's play-act Narcissus at the pond. Someone will be Narcissus. Narcissus looks at his reflection in the pond and will not look up-- he or she just has his attention on himself or herself. Finally, we'll pick some other people to try to help Narcissus look up from the pond, using the clues. And we'll need someone to play Echo.

"The helpers will do things to try and get Narcissus to be with them, but Narcissus will refuse at first ... just like we often do when we are mad or un-happy. Then the last helper, Echo, will gently touch Narcissus on the shoulder (e.g.), and empathize in a friendly manner and offer friendship. This will get Narcissus to look up at last."

Theater Mechanics

Select three to five children. The first is Narcissus. The others try to get him or her to look up from the pond, by using one of the Clues. The first 2-3 people fail to convince Narcissus to look up, because Narcissus is persistent in his fascination, and Narcissus even pushes away help. But relationship's seniority to self-absorption is closer to reality and the helpers are more persistent than Narcissus in the end, and he or she looks up from the pond and gives thanks and a high five or hugs or some such congratulations to the helper(s). Repeat this play by choosing another Narcissus and group of children to play the roles of Narcissus, Echo and helpers. THEY LOVE PLAYING THIS!

Author at Sanchez Elementary, 1994

Now that you have made "selfishness" an ordinary phenomenon, **Ask:** *Can you think of a time you were selfish? Can you think of a time when you were thinking only of yourself (like Narcissus)? Can you think of a time you felt beyond yourself and considered the feelings of others?*

Write: a *short* story (I only require 150-250 words, depending on the children), titled,

"A Time I was like Narcissus" or "**A Time I Was Selfish**"

- In this story, you MUST include: where, when, who, what.
- You must use the terms: "selfish", "Narcissus/Narcissitic", "I looked up when _____"
- You must include feelings and a lesson.
- The **audience** is the teacher; the kids are telling the teacher a story.
- There MUST be about 20 words of **advice** to your friends and peers on how to help someone look up from themselves to relationship.

The single essential ingredient of good manners is a sensitive awareness of others. If you have that awareness, you have good manners. If you don't, you don't.
—Emily Post

Student Samples

A Time I Was Selfish by Johnny

When I was in preschool, Remo brought a really cool toy for show and tell. So I got up and took it. But then I look up from the pond. I said I was sorry and he said, "OK." Then I asked if he wanted to be friends and he said "OK". We've been friends ever since. Over the years, he has given me a lot of things and has spent an amazing amount of money on me and I like to think I have done the same for him. But it's not about the toys or the clothes. It's about the friendship I made that wonderful day.

A Time I was Narcissus by Aidan

Last Summer my mom, brother, and I went to 7-11 one day. We went inside and I got Bubblicious gum, while my brother got a different type of gum. After, we hopped in the car and he asked if he could have a piece of my gum since mine was a new flavor. In return, he would share a piece of his gum with me. I was Narcissistic and said, "No, you have your own." But I thought about it for a little while and finally gave my brother a piece. (His gum was better.) I should have never been captured by the pond just for a piece of gum.

A Time I was Narcissus by Yasmeen

Last Friday at Seven Eleven I bought hot Cheetos. When I got back home my neighbor came over and she loves hot cheetos--but I didn't want to share. So I was so Narcissistic hid my Cheetos in my mom's cooking pot! But then I looked up from my little pond and got up and got the Cheetos out to share with her. I learned that if you are Narcissus you should look up from the pond and get up and share.

Narcissus by Sergio

Last summer my cousin and I got into a fight because I didnt get to play with the white house for the dolls, after a couple minutes, I left her and went to play my gamecube. My cousin wanted to play, but I didn't let her so she couldn't have fun. I looked up from the pond feeling my selfishness. I told my cousin, "You can play, I was just being a jerk, yeah sure you can play." I felt happy and proud and not like a brat. (I still got into a couple of fights later.)

Narcissus Story by Marcus

Once when I was 9, I had some friends over my house I was playing my video games my friends were begging me to play. My friends wanted to go home then I looked up from my pond of selfish behavior then I let them play longer than I did. Then we shared the video games then we were even better friends. Now every time I have a friend over I let them play my video games before me.

Teacher Preparation: Daedalus or Icarus?

Children readily contact great sources of energy, but as anyone can tell you, they often have a difficult time conducting it properly. They can learn however, to be energetic without being wild, if they have been compassionately taught. In a world built on stimulation we must also allow and encourage our children to learn balance, even-handedness, and even calm. This can be a challenge for the children, but it begins by understanding the difference between conducting energy with even-handedness or unconsciously **following** our impulsive wildness. By providing this understanding, we challenge them to grow toward this energetic, even-handed balance and to be conscious with our impulses.

This "even-handedness" in ancient Greek was "Daedalus"—usually used in reference to a masterful craftsmen and the skillful execution of their art. (*Daedalae*, like *Smith* today, was a common surname.) Even-handedness is the moral of the story of the great craftsman Daedalus and his impulsive son Icarus (whose name means "following").

Just as the story of Midas illustrates a lesson about true happiness and the story of Narcissus shows a lesson about unhappiness, the juxtaposition of Daedalus' evenhandedness and Icarus mindlessly following his every desire demonstrates the lesson of being balanced and of being unconsciously impulsive.

The bird is the primary symbol of the flowing (flying) feeling-attention, whether steady or impulsive. Daedalus is the archetype of conscious responsibility relative to being simple and steady when feeling "flies", and portrays the symbol for "even-handedness"; Icarus, likewise, is the archetype of unconsciously following an emotional expansion and its resultant lesson. By unconsciously zooming up and then crashing down into the sea, Icarus, in classic Greek sensibility, illustrates the tragic of character flaw of impulsive, non-mastery.

When children play, they can get a bit wild and un-controlled. Almost all their accidents occur while they are zooming around a bit too crazy — like Icarus! When accidents do occur, ask the children how they were being like Icarus. This story and lesson will help them to see the wisdom of being more like Daedalus — focused and not so wild. Likewise, when you see inappropriate, uncontrolled activity, you can prevent accidents from occurring by pointing out to your children that they are playing like Icarus, and that, if they don't calm down a bit and become more steady like Daedalus, somebody might crash.

Because children tend to see in black and white, take care not to make calm "good" and impulsiveness "bad". Point out that Icarus **unconsciously** followed his impulse, without thinking much about it. It is OK, even good, to follow impulses when you are conscious and thinking about it. And Daedalus wasn't just calm and boring; he was flying!

Hellenic: *Daedalus and Icarus*

The story of Daedalus and Icarus is a classic Hellenic myth, used here to illustrate the difference between masterful evenness and following your own impulsiveness.

Once upon a time, on the island of Crete, a great King named Minos wanted a magnificent garden around his palace. He sent for the famous craftsman Daedalus to design and construct the gardens. Daedalus came with his son, Icarus, who was learning from his father about craftsmanship.

Daedalus decided to build the gardens in a labyrinth—which is a puzzle that you try to find your way through. When the gardens were complete, King Minos loved them, but most people lost their way trying to walk through the maze. He even imprisoned his enemies there because they would spend their whole life trying to find their way out.

Once, Daedalus helped one of King Minos' foes get free from the labyrinth, so the King put Daedalus and his son under arrest. They were not allowed to board any ships in his harbor, and to swim to the next island would be too far. They would have to stay, or so the King thought. But the renowned craftsman Daedalus was not dismayed. He began building two sets of huge wings, one for himself and one for his son, Icarus.

Once Daedalus had constructed the lightweight frames for their arms, he and his son gathered feathers to put on the wings. Carefully gluing all the feathers on the

wings with wax, they worked every second of the day, and soon they were ready.

He warned his son, "Fly evenly and steadily like the eagle, and don't fly too high, or the sun will melt the wax." Then they put on their giant wings and began to fly! Daedalus and his son glided over the ocean like birds, happy and free.

Even though Daedalus reminded Icarus to be focused and careful, the boy soon became so excited that he started zooming around crazily and wildly. Sure enough, Icarus forgot what his father had told him and finally zoomed so high that the sun melted the wax on his wings, the feathers fell off, and he plummeted into the ocean.

****

Write: "Accidental" Stories

After you have engaged the short story of Daedalus and Icarus, then ask for volunteers to talk about a time they had an accident *because they were 'not-even' like Daedalus but crazy like Icarus*. Everyone has "war stories"; they love to share them!

Have all the children write a simple one-page reflection (I usually assign this for homework): "A Time I was like Icarus" (and had an accident). Use this simple assignment to practice **sensual descriptions and setting**, transition words, as well as **plain, silver and golden sentences**. Afterwards, share your exciting collection of "war stories" and point out the difference between careful "even-handedness" and following your impulses thoughtlessly.

*****

Student Sample:

About a week ago I said to my sister, "I bet you I can climb higher than you can on the tree." So she said, "Let's see."

So we went outside and I thought it would be easy for me since she is only six. So I started to climb up as fast as I could go so it would be over with, but when I was not high up, I slipped and fell, but I did not hurt myself a lot. But when my sister tried she focused and almost got to the top and beat me.

Cause I was being Icarus and she was being Daedalus.

Martin, San Anselmo, CA (age 9)

Core Stories is a companion volume to *Big Philosophy* and contains similar stories from around the world. I always have the children read the rest of the *Core Stories* in this section and invite an in-class appreciation. When there is time, I invite a compare-contrast analysis. I often see these stories referred to in other writings for the rest of the year.

It is easier to build strong children than to repair broken adults...
-Frederick Douglass-

Unit Five: Response-Ability
The Responsive Paragraph; Breath and Feeling

Responding to Quotes

The Concluding Sentence

The Juxtaposed Tales of Damonia and Destiny

The Inspirational Interplay of Breath and Feeling

Art Appreciation and Poetry

Common Core Standards Addressed

<u>Writing</u> 1a,b, c, d, 2c, e, 5, 10

<u>Reading Literature</u> 2, 4, 9, 10

<u>Reading Informational Text</u> 1, 2, 9

<u>Writing</u> 3b, d

<u>Writing</u> Narratives 3a, b, c, d, e, 5

The Responsive Paragraph

R-E-S-P-O-N-D
to Quotable Quotes

&

<u>Concluding Sentences</u>
(or "Teaching to the QWIER")

Kudos to Anne Diskin and Pat Endsley for these useful tools.

Making Writing Fun!

Responsive Paragraph Construction
R-E-S-P-O-N-D to Quotable Quotes

In the following unit, children are to pick a different quote every night from one of the pages of quotes (some pages may be "visited" more than once) and write **five** sentences in **response** to that quote. To give them support, lead them through the "RESPOND" legend (and see worksheet below):

R is for "Rephrase", could you say it another way? Is there a similar famous quote? Synonyms?

E is for "Example or Explain", This is an Example of _____; This means _____;

S is for "Summarize";

P is for "Parents" or "Peers";

O is for Opposite or Opinion;

N is for Note first thoughts;

D is for Describe (see following worksheet suggestions).

These <u>ten</u> prompts will give them ideas about how to write <u>five</u> sentences. I tell the children, "Make it easy, if you want, just ask your parents what they think — and write what they say." And let them know: they can add or substitute their own (or parent's) quotable quote to the list and write about *that*. They can write more than one sentence in each category, just write five sentences!

I let them know that *at first* it may be easy to start with "N": e.g., "The first "thing I **noted**, or thought of when I read this quote was...." They can easily transition to "E" for Explain, etc. Tell them they will be do this writing for three weeks, writing one responsive paragraph every homework-night.

The first two or three days, I have them list and label each sentence "R", "N", "P", "O", whatever (order is <u>not</u> important). As they turn in the first few assignments, I read them aloud to the class (anonymously) and praise and critique their efforts. This gives the whole class the kind of **feedback** that lets them know what is expected.

Once this basic sense of response is established, I then require the five sentences to be in paragraph form, without the "R", "N", "P", "O", etc. designation. Again, the only "correcting" I do is to through read-alouds with critiques and praises. I have the children practice this simple paragraph form for another week.

After a week or two, the children gain a basic facility in generating sentences in response to quotes, so then I help them **tighten** their paragraphs by focusing on the **final sentence**. For three days, they are to write five RESPOND sentences <u>and</u> five "QWIER" *concluding* sentences as well (see below) -- and *then* they **circle** the concluding sentence they think fits best with their RESPOND sentences (See both the RESPOND and the QWIER sentence-generator-prewrites below). After several days of five responsive sentences **and** five concluding sentences, they then **practice writing simple paragraphs**, five RESPOND sentences and one concluding QWIER sentence.

After these three weeks of practice, they then select one new quote and write <u>three</u> paragraphs about it-- using the skills they gained in the previous three weeks. These mini-essays are taken through an exhaustive writing process so that they shine. These can be made into a nice class book and/or bulletin board.

Concluding Sentences, or "Teaching to the QWIER" (pronounced "choir")

Emphasize how important it is to learn how to make a point again and again in many ways. That's why we write more than one sentence! Presenting and re-presenting (and re-presenting) an idea is one of the best writing skills anyone can learn.

After this review, tell the children that they are going to learn to make their paragraphs "tight" (insert current "cool" word) by teaching them how to make a powerful ending. A final concluding sentence wraps up the paragraph like a present!

Since the concluding sentence is often the weakest part of paragraph writing, I have the students exercise and practice this in isolation. First, I have them write a simple responsive paragraph, skip several lines, and then write <u>5</u> kinds of concluding sentences (from which they'll select their favorite).

I use the mnemonic device **QWIER** to prompt my kids to learn five kinds of concluding sentences. (Sample follows.)

Q stands for question. — Ask your reader a question that evokes the point of the paragraph.
W stands for Wish. — Make a "wish statement" that restates a salient point.
I stands for "If ..., then..." — Remind them to use proper punctuation (with the comma).
E stands for Exclamation! — Remind them to make a loud restatement with the proper punctuation.
R stands for Restatement (with synonyms). — Best practice technique here. Show them how they can Restate their topic sentence, trading as many words as possible with synonyms from a Thesaurus. (You'll need to give examples and then ask the class to participate in a few more.)

An example of five concluding sentences from a student:

Boom! That's the main sound on the 4th of July. The Fourth of July is the celebration of the birth of the nation, or the Declaration of Independence. The Declaration of Independence was written to show we are a nation of our own, and I <u>love</u> that. I also like the fireworks!
[possible concluding sentences...]
Q: I wonder if Thomas Jefferson was this happy?
W: I sure wish we celebrated like this more often.
I: If Thomas Jefferson were alive, then I think he would be sooo happy.
E: The 4th of July rocks!
R: Independence Day is the loudest and funnest holiday.

R-E-S-P-O-N-D

Rephrase. Can you say it another way? How would you say it another way? Is there a similar quote? What are the **synonyms** of the main words?

Explain/**E**xample. What does it mean? Can you give an example?

Summarize. Can you think of another saying that says the same kind of thing?

Parents, Peers. Ask the adults and friends in your life. What do they say about this?

Opposite/**O**ffer Your **O**pinion. What would the Opposite of this quote be? How do you agree? Is there a time or place you wouldn't agree?

Note Your Thoughts What was the first thing you thought of when you read it? How does the quote make you feel?

Describe. What might have been going on in their life or the world that moved them to say the quote?

Date:

NAME:

R	E	S	P	O	N	D
Rephrase	**Explain/ Example**	**Summarize**	**Parents/ Peers**	**Opposite/ Offer Your Opinion**	**Note Your Thoughts**	**Describe**
Can you say it another way? What are the synonyms of the main words?	What does it mean? What would be an example of this?	Can you summarize or think of another saying that says the same kind of thing?	Ask the adults or friends in your life. What do they say about this?	What would be the opposite of this? Is there a time or place you wouldn't agree?	What was the first thing you thought of when you read it? How does the quote make you feel?	What was going on in their life (or in the world) that moved them to say the quote?

Selected Quote _____

_____

(Alternative Chart)

Teaching to the QWIER
Powerful Concluding Sentences

Q stands for question. -- Ask the reader a question that evokes the point of the paragraph.

W stands for Wish. --- Make a "wish statement" that restates a salient point.

I stands for "If ..., then..."

E stands for Exclamation! A loud restatement.

R stands for Restatement (<u>with synonyms</u>). Restate the topic sentence, trading as many words

as possible with synonyms.

Quotable Quotes Categories

THE GOLDEN CIRCLE OF BEHAVIOR AND EXPERIENCE

EXCELLENCE

SELF KNOWLEDGE

THE POWER OF THOUGHT

PERCEPTION

SPEECH

RESTRAINT

MIND

APPRECIATION

SERVICE

YOUR FAVORITES

THE GOLDEN CIRCLE OF BEHAVIOR AND EXPERIENCE

The only way to have a friend is to be a friend.
— Ralph Waldo Emerson

As you give, so shall you receive.
— Books of both Mathew and Luke

Ingratitude is sooner or later fatal to its author.
— Twi (West African) proverb

Tse-king asked, "Is there one word which may serve
as a rule of practice for all of one's life?"
The Master said, "Is not **reciprocity** such a word?"
— Confucius

The way you prepare the bed, so shall you sleep.
— Yiddish proverb

What goes around, comes around.

Treat others as you would like others to treat you.

Use wisely your power of choice.
— Og Mandino

EXCELLENCE

Better to do a little well, than a great deal badly.
— Sokrates

What is defeat? Nothing but an education,
the first step to something better.
— Wendell Phillips

You never really lose until you stop trying.
— Mike Ditka

Failing to plan is planning to fail.
— Ben Franklin

The price of greatness is responsibility.
— Winston Churchill

In the long run, you hit only what you aim at.
Therefore, though you should fail,
immediately you had better aim at something high.
— Henry David Thoreau

EXCELLENCE II

First honesty, then industry, then concentration.
— Andrew Carnegie

Winning is great, sure, but if you want to do something in life,
the secret is learning how to lose. Nobody goes undefeated
all the time, but if you can pick yourself up after a defeat
and go on to win again, you can be a champion.
— Wilma Rudolph

I find that the harder I work, the more luck I seem to have.
— Thomas Jefferson

The will to win is worthless if you do not have the will to prepare.
— Louis Pasteur

Excellence is the gradual result of always striving to do better.
—Pat Riley

Quality in not an act, it is a habit.
— Aristotle

SELF KNOWLEDGE

An unexamined life is not worth living. Know yourself.
— Sokrates

God gives nothing to those who keep their arms crossed.
— Bam Bara (West African proverb)

A person should never stop learning, even on their last day.
— Maimonides

Try not to be a person of success,
but rather try to become a person of value.
— Albert Einstein

People who laugh actually live longer than those who don't laugh.
Few persons realize that health actually varies
according to the amount of laughter.
— James D. Walsh, M.D.

With lies you may go ahead in the world-
but you can never go back.
— Russian proverb

SELF KNOWLEDGE II

We are what we repeatedly do. We do not act rightly
because we have virtue or excellence, but we rather have virtue
because we have acted rightly.
— Aristotle

A good reputation is more valuable than money.
— Publilius Syrus

Honesty is the first chapter in the book of wisdom.
— Thomas Jefferson

He who forgives ends the quarrel.
— West African proverb

The knowledge of self is the mother of all knowledge.
— Kahil Gibran

I think self-knowledge is the rarest trait in a human being.
— Elizabeth Edwards

SELF KNOWLEDGE III

The wise person looks within their heart and finds
the peace that does not pass.
— Hindu proverb

A person can fail many times, but they aren't a failure until
they begin to blame others.
— Ted Engstrom

Worry affects the circulation, the heart, the glands,
the whole nervous system, and profoundly affects the health.
I have never known a man who died from overwork,
but many who died from doubt.
— Charles W. Mayo

If you are facing the right direction, all you need
to do is keep walking.
— Buddhist proverb

Within infinity, we are small. Know your self thusly.
— Upon the Temple at Delphi

THE POWER OF THOUGHT

We are the result of what we have thought.
— Gautama Shakyamuni

You are today where your thoughts have brought you.
You will be tomorrow where your thoughts take you.
— James Allen

Your thoughts are like boomerangs.
— Eileen Caddy

If there is no dull and determined effort,
there will be no brilliant achievement.
— Hsun-tze

As you think, so are you. Thoughts are things;
therefore, think the things that will make the world better
and you unashamed.
— Henry H. Buckley

Whether you think you can or you can't, you're right.
— Henry Ford

You become what you meditate upon.
— Adi Da

PERCEPTION

The appearance of things changes according to the emotion.
— Kahil Gibran

A person is what they believe.
— Anton Chekhov

We do not see things as they are, we see things as we are.
— Talmud

Those who cannot feel the littleness of great things in themselves
are apt to overlook the greatness of little things in others.
— Kakuzo Okakura

A man hears what he wants to hear, and disregards the rest.
— Paul Simon

A pessimist sees the difficulty in every opportunity;
an optimist sees the opportunity in every difficulty.
— Sir Winston Churchill

How you look is not as important as how you see.
— Frank Marrero

SPEECH

Good words are worth much and cost little.
— George Herbert

Speech is the mirror of the soul; as a person speaks, so they are.
— Publilius Syrus

A person is seldom better than their conversation.
— German proverb

Gentle speech makes friends.
— Wisdom of Sirach

Language exerts hidden power, like the moon on the tides.
— Rita Mae Brown

The instruments of both life and death
are contained within the power of the tongue.
— Judaic proverb

A person's speech about others
is often a reflection of themselves.
— Frank Marrero

One kind word can warm three winter months.
— African Proverb

RESTRAINT

Restraint does not mean weakness. It does not mean giving in.
— Jawaharlal Nehru

There is none better than self-restraint.
— Lao Tzu

A person without self-restraint is like a barrel without hoops,
and tumbles to pieces.
— Henry Ward Beecher

If you are patient in one moment of anger,
you will escape a hundred days of sorrow.
— Chinese proverb

No person is free who is not a master of themselves.
— (ascribed to many) Epictetus, Pythagoras, Siddhartha, Confucius

When restraint and courtesy are added to strength,
the latter becomes irresistible.
— Mahatma Gandhi

MIND

Chance favors the minds which are prepared.
— Louis Pasteur

A good mind is lord of a kingdom.
— Seneca

There will always be a frontier where there is an open mind
and a willing hand.
— Charles F. Ketterling

If passion drives you, let reason hold the reins.
— Benjamin Franklin

What this power is I cannot say;
all I know is that it exists and it becomes available only
when a man is in that state of mind in which he knows exactly
what he wants and is fully determined not to quit until he finds it.
— Alexander Graham Bell

APPRECIATION

To be upset over what you don't have
is to waste what you do have.
— Ken Keyes

Do not delay; the golden moments fly!
— Henry Wadsworth Longfellow

Outward beauty is transient, but inner beauty lasting.
— Seyyed Hossein Nasr

We can become bitter or better.
— Eric Butterworth

I say: Go outside into the field, nature and the sun, go out
and find the mystery in yourself and in God.
Think of the beauty that again and again expresses itself
with you and outside of you and be happy.
— Anne Frank

Joy is not in things, but is in you.
— John Templeton

Don't underrate, appreciate.
—Jon Anderson

SERVICE

Everyone can be great because everyone can serve.
— Martin Luther King, Jr.

The end of all education should surely be service to others.
— Cesar Chavez

The high destiny of the individual is to serve rather than to rule.
— Albert Einstein

The best way to find yourself
is to lose yourself in the service of others.
— Mahatma Gandhi

If you want happiness for a lifetime - help the next generation.
— Chinese Proverb

Men are rich only as they give.
He who gives great service gets great rewards.
— Elbert Hubbard

In nothing do men approach so nearly to the gods
as doing good to others.
— Cicero

MISCELLANEOUS

Doubts and jealousies often beget the fact they fear.
— Thomas Jefferson

Present fears are less than horrible imaginings.
— William Shakespeare

He who never makes mistakes never makes anything.
— English proverb

If you shut your doors to all errors, truth will be shut out.
— Rabindranath Tagore

The strongest principle of growth lies in human choice.
— George Elliot

I have found the paradox that if I love until it hurts,
then there is not hurt, but only more love.
— Mother Theresa

Excuses satisfy only those that give them.
&
Only the boring get bored.
—on the front of my classroom

(Make Your Own Favorites Here)

The Four Great Voices Paragraph
(optional/advanced)

Another type of responsive paragraph incorporates the Four Great Voices: "I" (opinion), "It" (fact), "We" (meaning), and "All" (context or summary). Please see the pre-write on the next page.. To exercise this kind of responsive paragraph, the student puts the main idea in the center of the pre-write, then uses the **sentence starters** to respond to the main idea from four different points of view.

This Four Great Voices Paragraph is a classic example of what is meant by an "**Integral**" curriculum. It is an "integral" program not because it integrates multiple subject areas, but because it addresses the human being in personal and social domains, in behaviorial as well as feeling dimensions.

For my fuller elaboration of "integral", especially as it applies to elementary education, please see the Appendix: "An Integral Approach to Affective Education" (and published in Ken Wilber's *AQAL Journal*).

Student Sample

My favorite part of the Preamble to the Constitution is "to secure the blessings of liberty to ourselves and posterity". I feel that it is important to have liberty and freedom because then we can all be equal. Many people say that they want liberty and not one ruler with all the power. It is a fact that if we have liberty, there will be more peace. All together, we need liberty so we can have peace.

The Four Great Voices Paragraph Pre-Write

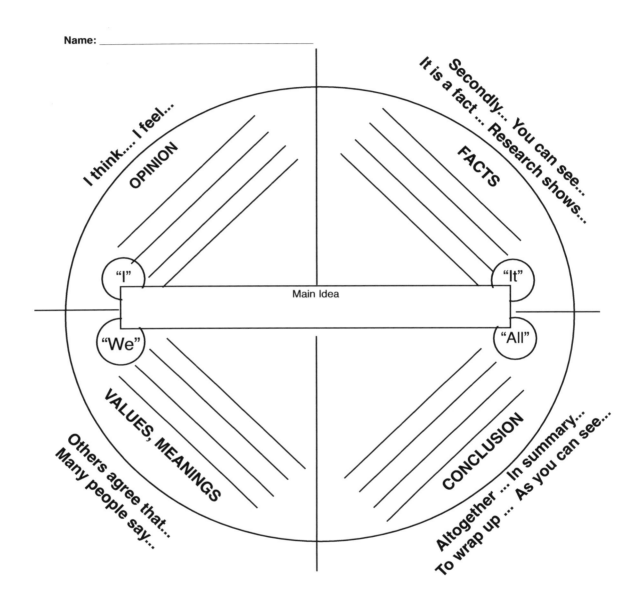

Name: _____

I think.... I feel...

OPINION

Secondly... You can see...
It is a fact ... Research shows...

FACTS

"I"

"It"

Main Idea

"We"

"All"

VALUES, MEANINGS

Others agree that...
Many people say...

CONCLUSION

Altogether ... In summary...
To wrap up ... As you can see...

Damonia and Destiny:
The Juxtaposed Tales of Twin Sisters

This is a review lesson on two fronts: one, to once again practice setting, character, plot, and message; two, to revisit moral choices. Here we also practice using quotes, where the student must choose a quote and have a character in the story quote it (suggestions are given). You may copy the following page as a hand-out to help students get into the different characters.

Thank you Jordon for being so so great!

Damonia   **and**   **Destiny**

1. If you said, "How's it going?", how do you think each would respond?

2. If you said, "I lost my favorite game," what do you think would be different about the responses from each sister?

3. If you said, "Where do you live" or "I like....................., what do you like?", what kind of responses could you imagine from each one?

4. How do they do in school?

5. What are they like in the class and on the playground?

What other questions can you imagine you could ask to see the difference in their character?

Answering these questions will give you some of the basic ingredients for writing two good short stories.

Writing Assignment

Write two short stories.

The first paragraph containing the set up and setting for both is exactly the same: You and Damonia (then you and Destiny) happen to be walking along (from where, to where, why were you together? **Sensually** describe the day) and you come upon a purse (or satchel or bag) full of money.

What happens? What do you and D _____agree upon? disagree upon? What happens?

Write at least three scenes for each choice, sensually describing each one. Include back and forth dialogue in every scene. Have them self-edit themselves using the rubric on the next page. Then, before they turn it in, they do a "read aloud" to a partner (in turn), and check their evaluation with a classmate (in turn).

Before they do their next rewrite, review figurative language. Require them to **practice** including all three kinds of sentences: Plain-Silver-Gold (review the Chart).

Quotable Quotes Quota: Select from the following quotes to use in some way. Have a character quote them, say, "As [Famous Person] says, ..." Or just have one character say it.

A good reputation is more valuable than money.
Publilius Syrus

The way you prepare the bed, so shall you sleep.
Yiddish proverb

What goes around, comes around.

Restraint does not mean weakness. It does not mean giving in.
Jawaharlal Nehru

Honesty is the first chapter in the book of wisdom.
Thomas Jefferson

Checklist for Damonia and Destiny Stories

SCENE ONE
First Setting

___Time of Day, Time of Year
___2 Things you can see
___1 thing you can hear
___1 extra sensation (temperature, smell, taste, or excellent detail?)
___A Feeling

Character

___gender/age/size/shape
___color of hair, skin, eyes
___color and style or clothes
___body language, "eyes (color!) seemed to be saying, _____"
___INTRODUCE PROBLEM

SCENE TWO (Rising Action)
Second Setting

___2 Things you can see
___1 thing you can hear
___1 extra sensation (temperature, smell, taste, or excellent detail?)
___A Feeling

Minor Character

___gender/age/size/shape
___color of hair, skin, eyes
___color and style or clothes
___body language, "eyes (color!) seemed to be saying, _____"

SCENE THREE (resolution)
Third Setting

___2 Things you can see
___1 thing you can hear
___1 extra sensation (temperature, smell, taste, or excellent detail?)
___A Feeling

3rd Character

___gender/age/size/shape
___color of hair, skin, eyes
___color and style or clothes
___body language, "eyes (color!) seemed to be saying, _____"

The Inspired Interplay of Breath and Feeling

The smoke of my own breathing

echoes, ripples buzz'd whispers

love-root, silk thread,

my respiration and inspiration,

the beating of my heart,

the passing of blood and air

through my lungs.

—Walt Whitman

There is one way of breathing

that is shameful and constricted.

Then there's another way:

a breath of love that takes you

all the way to infinity.

—Rumi

The Transformation of Psyche

While *psyche* was commonly used as the ancient Greek word for "soul", what is rarely pointed out is that this word is rooted in *psychein*, "to breathe". In the Western cultures particularly, we have forgotten this ancient understanding of the intertwining of breath and feeling — and we usually make fun of what we do not understand rationally. Yet even our modern culture has acknowledged this common observation: if you are feeling bad, take a breath or two, it will help; if you are feeling fine, take a breath or few and you will magnify your happiness. To help transform feeling, use the breath.

The following stories from ancient Africa and Greece serve to help the children learn the value of accentuating aspects of the breath to aid in specific emotional situations. Just as it is good to exercise the body for strength, likewise it is good and necessary to exercise the breathing, feeling, and emotional capacity of the individual. The breath exercises in this section are primarily intended for the seven- to twelve-year-old group, for whom the feeling dimension is the focus of attention and development, but they can be adapted with some success to breathers of all ages.

*****

When the children do their create-comprehension exercise for the story of Pharoh Zoser, have them include the following questions:

1. To balance the emotion of sadness or sorrow, what part of the breath do you accentuate?
2. To balance the emotion of fear, what parts of the breath do you accentuate?

After you collect their Create Comprehensions, post the **Royal Breaths Chart** (page 152). Ask the children what is the part of the breath that is accentuated for anger and frustration. I often have the children dramatize or "fake" each emotion (pretending to be scared/sad/angry), then ask them to first feel the tightness or sensation in the body, then ask them to practice the corresponding breath and see how much it helps. Point out that it often takes many breaths to melt away the sadness or madness or fear, but the natural feeling will come back sooner with the help of the breath.

Vocabulary for "The Death of Pharoh Zoser"

vizier   _____

immortality_____

physician   _____

sorrowful   _____

inspired   _____

resonance   _____

jackal   _____

African: The Death of Pharoh Zoser
This is a fictionalized account of real personalities (2686 B.C.E.),

The Great Pharoh Zoser was dying and so he asked for his friend and vizier, Imhotep, who was also the wisest man in all the world, to come to him. The Pharoh had long prepared for his death with prayer, self-reflection, and good works. He built the first great step pyramid, jewel of Africa, designed by Imhotep, to carry him into immortality. Even still, Pharoh Zoser was afraid.

When Imhotep stepped into the Royal Chambers, the Pharoh praised him, "They call you master magician, master physician, master astronomer, master architect, master builder. They call you Master; I am lucky to call you my friend."

Imhotep smiled lovingly at his friend and Pharaoh. They grasped each other's hand in deep friendship and Imhotep kissed the dark skin of his beloved Pharoh. Before Imhotep could speak, Zoser continued to praise him, "Even as a child, you loved learning, and now you are the wisest man in all the world. Tell me again, my friend, about the test in the afterlife: the Breath of Life, the Hall of Judgement, and Spirit Feather of Ma'at. I am dying ... my heart is sorrowful, and I am afraid." The Pharoh asked Imhotep to guide him through his dying process.

Imhotep, 'he who comes in peace', looked at his dying friend and held his hand. He thought of his own childhood and how lucky he had been to develop a passion for learning. Imhotep thought of all his studies; his mathematics, his designs, his star charts, his medical mastery, his collection of wise and inspired sayings. And now, none of that mattered more than holding his dying friend's hand and helping him with a few last breaths to embrace the harmonic Ma'at. The Ma'at was harmony, felt as balance, well-being, and spirit. Ma'at's patterns of harmony could be seen with the eyes as beauty, heard by the ears as heartful tones, felt in the body, breath, and mind as the current of life. Harmonic Ma'at could be seen in patterns and numbers, in nature, and in all arts. By feeling the Ma'at of anything, one could feel the truth of anything as well.

"Don't worry, my Pharoh," Imhotep assured him, "to die is as natural as living. Long after our pyramid has turned into sand, the royal breaths will carry the wise into the wonderful truth."

The Pharoh remembered Imhotep's lessons on Ma'at; he remembered the resonance of all things and beings. Surrendering to the feeling of Ma'at had been his practice everyday.

The tension in the Pharoh's body melted away, and a smile broke across his face. "Yes, but let me hear one more time, from your sweet lips, the art of passing through the Hall of Truth."

Imhotep could tell that Pharoh Zoser was dying in his arms. He held his pharoh and held back his tears, whispering into his royal ear, "Let go, my friend, let go. Let go of all that you regret doing, let go of all you regret not doing, let go. Let your dying be easy, let go to easy death, like falling into sweet sleep. Let go with your royal breaths; sigh and let go, let go as you sigh, let go. Breathe deeply and surrender to Ma'at's harmony." Imhotep reassured his royal friend, "Beauty is everywhere; everything is aglow with spirit, we are happy with you, love you, thank you. Breathe deeply and let go, relax completely and surrender."

Imhotep could feel how his Pharoh was following his words, following his heart, following the spirit. Imhotep watched a tear roll down the royal face, revealing a sadness within. "Remember the royal breaths for the clouds of sadness; just blow them away. The Sun Ra, the light inside, is always shining. Smile inwardly as you blow away the clouds of sadness; smile inwardly and breathe the Bright Ra light."

A lightness filled the royal chambers, but as Pharoh Zoser began to die, he clutched at Imhotep's hand, and the rising lightness stalled. Imhotep held his Pharoh more tightly and guided him beyond. "Breathe evenly, and you can melt the frozen fear." Imhotep was silent while the Pharoh took a long, slow breath. "Breathe deeply and feel the breath of life melting your fears. Breathe evenly and deeply, and feel the breath of life making your heart as light as a feather. Breathe the breath of life and let go to heart-happiness. The presence in the heart is the universal radiance of the eternal being, and the core of everything and everyone, appearing and disappearing in the heart's wondrous light."

Zoser breathed deeply until a great happiness consumed him. Imhotep could see that the Pharoh had let go and called to him, "Soon you will come to the Hall of Truth, where Annubis, the jackal god of the dead, will weigh your heart against the weight of a feather. It is the Feather of Ma'at. Passing the test of Annubis, one becomes True of Voice, but if you do not, Beby, the destroyer, will devour you.

"Breathe deeply the Harmonic Ma'at. Breathe deeply the Spirit of Light in your heart," Imhotep lovingly guided his pharoh. "Now that your heart is as light as a feather, you will pass the Hall of Truth into the Life which is eternal."

The royal chambers became all bright as the Pharoh fell into grateful rapture. Blessedly and blissfully his breathing was set free as it merged into a sudden wind. Imhotep kissed the Pharoah's forehead as Pharoh Zoser breathed no more.

Annubis Weighing the Heart of a Soul Against the Feather of Ma'at
Hungry Beby Awaits the Heavy Hearts, Scribe and Attendants Process the Judgement

Hellenic: Psyche

*This is a gathering of many Psyche stories with
the technicalities of the breath added to supplement the theme.*

Psyche was a princess of such remarkable beauty that everyone worshiped her as if she were Aphrodite, the goddess of beauty. Psyche enjoyed being praised so much that she forgot to give credit to Aphrodite, and soon Aphrodite's temples lay neglected. Everyone came to admire the king's daughter instead. This angered the true goddess of beauty, who decided to teach Psyche a lesson.

"How dare they call her beauty divine, when she is only a mortal and will die someday!" fumed Aphrodite, "What foolishness to worship that which rots!!" She called her winged son Eros, the god of love, to help her with her plan. Eros was famous for shooting divine arrows through the hearts of people and making them fall in love. Aphrodite instructed Eros to shoot Psyche when she was near an ugly man, making her fall in love, so that she would marry him and people would forget about her. Aphrodite sent Eros to the city where Psyche lived and told him, "There she is, the woman who is content to steal glory from a goddess. Wait for an ugly man and then shoot them both. This will avenge her pride!"

But as fate would have it, Eros was also taken by the sight of Psyche. He loved watching her. Yet when an ugly unhappy servant of the King came by, Eros began to follow his mother's instructions. He selected his most potent love-arrow and inserted it into his bow. He drew the arrow back, but as destiny had it, he pricked his own hand, and fell madly in love with Psyche himself.

Even though Psyche was famous for her beauty, no one had ever asked to marry her. Long after her less beautiful sisters had married and moved from home, Psyche still had not found any suitors. Her father, the King, wondered why and went to Delphi to ask the oracle of Apollo for help. He trusted that he would find wisdom in finding a husband for Psyche. As usual, the oracle spoke mysteriously,

"Let Psyche be clad as a corpse in mourning clothes,
set her on a lonely rock to await her destiny.
Her husband shall be no mortal but a winged wild creature."

146

Apollo's commandment was so strange that the King cried. Everyone who heard the news, including Psyche, felt shocked and assumed that she would be married to some sort of dragon! But they knew that they must follow the law or disaster would surely befall them all.

Soon, the day of her funeral-marriage arrived and though Psyche did not fight her destiny, she cried along with the King and Queen, and the whole town. When the procession came to the hilltop outside of town, Psyche hugged her mother and father goodbye. She could feel how she had been full of false pride and how this had angered Aphrodite. She tried to comfort her parents. "Please don't cry anymore or tear your hair with grief. We should have known when everyone called me Aphrodite that we would stir her anger. Let us accept what the heavens have given. I'm not afraid anymore."

Trembling but resigned, Psyche awaited the fulfillment of the oracle, seated on a solitary rock. Soon everyone left, fearful of the dragon that was to come. Night fell and Psyche passed into sleep.

Suddenly, she felt herself being gently lifted into the arms of the western wind Zephyrus, who carried her to a magnificent palace, surrounded by gardens and filled with flowers. It was in this sweet darkness that she heard a friendly voice speak to her. "All you see is for your enjoyment. Don't be afraid. Come take a bath and have some food. You will have everything you need." In the darkness she could see no one, even though she often heard the friendly voice that had helped her. So she explored the palace and found a bath freshly drawn and dinner ready for her. Psyche finally made her way to bed, and as she was on the verge of sleep, a mysterious being joined her in the darkness, explaining that he was the husband for whom she was destined. She could not see his features, but his voice was soft and his conversation full of tenderness. Before the return of dawn, the strange visitor disappeared, first making Psyche promise to never attempt to see his face. In spite of the oddness of the adventure, Psyche was not discontented with her new life; in the palace nothing she could desire was lacking except the constant presence of her delightful husband, who came to visit her only during the dark hours of the night.

Her happiness could have continued in this way if her sisters–who were consumed by envy–had not sown the seeds of suspicion in her heart. "If your husband is afraid to let you see his face," they said, "it is because he must really be some hideous monster." At first, Psyche told Eros of her sisters' suspicions and he charged her with faith, saying, "You must trust me, trust Love. Promise me." Psyche assured him that she felt his love and did not need to see his form. But her sisters nagged her so much

that one night Psyche, in spite of her promise, rose from the couch that she shared with her husband, secretly lighted a lamp and held it above the mysterious face. Instead of a fearful monster she beheld the most charming person in the world—Eros himself. At the foot of the couch lay his bow and arrows. In her delight Psyche held the lamp nearer in order to study her husband's features more closely. A drop of scalding oil fell on the god's bare shoulder. He was hurt and awakened at once, realizing that Psyche had broken her promise and the faith between them. He flew away without a word, landing momentarily in a tree, calling back, "Am I a monster or your saviour? Did I seem

like a beast to you? My heart is as hurt as my shoulder. You will be sufficiently punished by my absence. I will pray that my mother will not destroy you." Holding his wound, he set his wings in motion and flew away.

The palace vanished simultaneously, and poor Psyche found herself on a lonely rock again in terrifying solitude. She began to wander the countryside looking for Eros, but he was in Olympia healing his wound. Psyche wanted to die and threw herself into a near-by river, but the waters bore her gently to the opposite bank. From then on she was pursued by Aphrodite's anger and had to pass a series of terrible ordeals. Aphrodite brought Psyche to a room and dumped urns of lentils, poppy seeds, barley, and sesame seeds in a pile on the floor and told Psyche, "You must have all the seeds sorted and back in the right urns by nightfall."

At first, Psyche collapsed and didn't know what to do. But then she took a big breath and with tears in her eyes, she finally began her task, focusing her attention on picking up a single grain at a time. Then, mysteriously, an ant appeared who told her that he and his friends would help. By sunset they had put all the seeds back into their proper urns. Aphrodite fumed and gave her another impossible test. She told Psyche to gather a single cup of water from a high mountain stream guarded by a monster. Again, Psyche was initially dismayed but, once again, took a deep breath and began her journey, trusting that she would succeed. Suddenly, an eagle swooped down, picked up the cup from her with its talons, and flew to the pure and high icy stream. The monster could not touch the eagle as it swooped down and filled the cup.

Aphrodite then gave Psyche the most difficult task of all. She sent Psyche into the Underworld to get a cup of beauty from Persephone, Queen of the Dead. To pass into the underworld without dying was practically impossible.

Guarding the entrance was the three-headed monster dog named Cerebus, but Psyche was so calmed by her breathing that her beauty shone even in the darkness and so the monstrous Cerebus just sat in awe as she passed by. The cold-hearted ferryman Charon, who takes souls across the river Styx, likewise, was so charmed by Psyche that he too simply served her.

As Psyche descended into Hades, she became angry at Aphrodite for making her do all of these things, and stamped her feet in anger. But she was a princess, and she understood that her royal teacher had taught her to use the royal breaths in any difficult encounter. She noticed how in anger she felt like exploding and all of her feeling wanted to rush *out*. Her royal knowledge of proper breaths taught her how to balance the energy of any bad feeling. So instead of exploding, she thought about how much graceful help she had already received and concentrated on breathing that feeling *in*. With several breaths the anger had dissolved and she was able to resume her journey downwards.

As she continued, she remembered her lost lover and became very sad, thinking that she would never feel loved again. But Psyche's strength came from a great depth and instead of crying, she noticed how she felt collapsed *in* and out of balance. So, to even out the collapsed feeling she breathed *out* very deeply, and told herself that, if she had another chance, she would trust love, instead of doubting it. She knew that she could blow away the clouds of sorrow from the sun of happiness with a few big breaths.

Soon she came to the Court of the Dead and made her request for a cup of beauty to Persephone. Hades glared at Psyche and screamed, "How dare you come into my kingdom alive?" He took up his sword to kill her.

Noticing her feeling was frozen, Psyche breathed evenly and as deeply as she could. She did not run or collapse, even though she trembled. Her faith and deep breaths caused Hades to pause inquisitively and ask her why she had come. Psyche told her story so openly that Persephone felt merciful, and gave her a jar of her own beauty creme.

Climbing back out of the Underworld was tiring and Psyche paused near the entrance back to earth. As she rested she was tempted to try just a touch of the beauty creme herself. She opened the jar and dipped her fingertip into Persephone's creme. Upon touching the magic substance she was overwhelmed and collapsed onto the earth at the portal of the underworld.

Eros, now healed from Psyche's wound, saw her lying unconscious on the ground and flew down to take her in his arms. For even though Psyche had betrayed him, Eros had been the secret voice that had helped her and that had instructed all the creatures and forces to assist and help her. He wiped away the sleep from her face and put it back into the box of beauty creme. He awakened her with a harmless prick from the tip of his arrow, and holding her in his arms he said, "You have almost perished from overmuch curiosity and fascination, but you passed the final test. Be well. Now go to my mother and give her the beauty. Tell her of your love for me and I will provide for all things, each in its right season."

The awakened princess fully embraced the husband of her heart, just as she had promised in the Underworld. Eros flew her skyward to the Court of Olympia to make peace with the goddess of beauty. In the heavenly abode they spoke with Aphrodite, and even Zeus spoke in their behalf.

"O ye Gods, you doubtless know this young god and my son, whom I have nourished with mine own hand. He is now bridled and has learned modesty. He has chosen a maiden that favors him well. Let him embrace Psyche." Then Zeus turned to Aphrodite and said, "And you, my daughter, do not fear any dishonor because Psyche is a mortal, for I will see to it that this marriage is equal and just."

Zeus took a pot of immortality and gave it to Psyche, saying, "Drink deeply that thou are made immortal, and may Eros never depart from you but be thine everlasting husband."

A sumptuous banquet and marriage feast appeared. Eros held his bride and they sat at the uppermost seat together. Dionysus served the drink of nectar, the Hours decked the house with flowers, Apollo's fingers moved freely upon the lyre as the Muses sang sweet harmony, and the Satyr's played the pan-pipes. Thus Psyche was married to Love and all the stars glistened.

*****

The Royal Breaths Chart

When you're not feeling well or happy,
intentionally STRENGTHEN some breaths,
and you will feel better.

*****

When you are **scared or nervous**,
your breath is frozen,
so take several EVEN and DEEP breaths.

*****

When you are **sad** or **bored**,
your feeling is collapsed,
but you can BLOW IT AWAY, breath after breath.

*****

When you are **angry** or **frustrated**,
your feeling is exploding,
but you can BALANCE anger
by BREATHING IN really big,
(and counting your blessings).

*****

When you are **happy**, your feeling is free
and you can ENERGIZE your body by
BREATHING HAPPINESS ALL THROUGH YOU.

Writing: Art Appreciation and Poetry

Every year, I took a field trip to an art museum in San Francisco where my students are engaged in the *Poets in the Gallery* program, led by Devorah Major. Ms. Major gathered the

children around various works of art (as below) and told them stories and facts about the piece. Then she engaged the children to "talk to the art" via a variety of modalities. For instance, she asked the children to describe **"living colors"** they see, BUT they cannot use the words "red", "orange", "yellow", "green", etc. These are replaced with associative words such as "watermelon", "golden", "setting sun", "clover", etc. She also requires the children to describe **"motion"** or **"action"** such as "standing stones", "rushing water" and the like. Martin Heidegger's poem is a good example of this:

> *Forests spread*
> *Brooks plunge*
> *Rocks persist*
> *Mist diffuses*
>
> *Meadows wait*
> *Springs well*
> *Winds dwell*
> *Blessing muses.*

Ms. Major asks the children to describe the **emotion** or **feeling** that the art contained or evoked. Of course, she insists on including **sensory details** in abundance. And she asked the children to talk to the art through a variety of **points of view**. For instance, the child could imagine that they were there with the artist as they were finishing the work and would complement him or her about several things. How would they tell the artist what they liked and why? Talk to the artist. Or the student can <u>be in the painting</u> or sculpture speaking to the student or to the artist from the painting/sculpture. What could they say?

This was one of those special occasions when I could actually feel the inner appreciation of the beauty of the moment passing like an electric current through the brush in my hand.
—Prince Charles

Writing: Museum Art and Poetry

Once the modalities of interchange with art are explored, have the children write poems, choosing point of iew, then "talk", using **Motion or Action, Emotion or Feelings, Sensory Details, Living Colors, Story,** and the like.

*****

Three Student Samples (Fifth grade)

(In participation with the Egyptian Art from the story of "The Death of King Zoser")

I smack my lips as we all curiously wait.

We wait in silence, in stillness

as everything is paused for a moment.

All the colors are faded and still.

We wait to see if the heart weighs less than the feather,

I hope not, for I shall devour it quickly and leave no mess.

I am nervous to see if I can eat.

My eyes are still and full of anger.

The heavy heart fears me because I am Beby!

Look at Beby's red blazing eyes.

Look at the angry disguise.

As I paint, I can feel the heart pounding with fear.

And now Beby's lunch is near.

Will the feather's end drop low?

Or perhaps the heart of the Pharoh?

But for now we shall wait

In the faded room full of hate.

I am the Feather of Ma'at

My color is so bright

I lie in a scale vs. the heart

as my white smooth feathers are weighed

against the heart of the Pharoh

I think, "Will he live in the eternal Life

Or be eaten by Beby?"

Now I know my Pharoh's heart is as light as me

He will pass through the Hall of Truth

and live in the Life that is and always will be eternal.

To create one's own world takes courage.
— Georgia O'Keeffe

Treat a work of art like a prince: let it speak to you first."
— Arthur Schopenhauer

Art is standing with one hand extended into the universe and one hand extended into the world,
and letting ourselves be a conduit for passing energy.
— Albert Einstein

I am my own experiment. I am my own work of art.
— Madonna

Tristan van Go, outside the Museum

Ms Major was brilliant

Unit Six: The Developmental Rainbow

Writing Full Essays On Growing Up, Exercising Parallelism and Personalizations

What Is It To Really Grow Up?

A Real Talk for Kids Today
about a Wonderful Future

Responsive Essay Writing
Focusing on Parallelism
(3-4 weeks)

Common Core Standards Addressed

<u>Writing</u> **2a, b, c, d, 3d, 5, 10**

There she was coming at me: The grandmother of a former student of mine who had invited me to his graduation. The problem was that Rick only had four tickets to the ceremony: one for his mom and dad (dispatcher and policeman), his dear sister, and, well, I got the ticket that granny was supposed to have.

Grandmother's furor was tempered by how I "had saved her grandson's life". She embraced me with gratitudes and humorous insults. Everyone's snickers and howls added to the honor I felt that Rick wanted me, seven years after our class. There was hearty laughter throughout the evening.

Rick relayed how he had learned from my lessons in Big Philosophy for Little Kids that when the "three-headed dragon of adolescence" would start to overtake him, he would recognize it and not be broken by doubt, depression, or dilemma.

Over the decades, my (writing) lessons on growing up, and particularly the Three-headed Dragon are the most common appreciation I receive from students-turned-adults. (The lessons on Midas and True Happiness and the investigations of Narcissus that I received from Adi Da are the other most appreciated lessons that my former students praise.)

Normalized within the real struggle of the adolescent passage, the images and telling promote the recognition whereby we need not be crushed by the monster of separativeness, with furies of abstraction, the alienation of mentality, and the aloneness of Narcissus.

When demons are recognized, the possibility for relationship, true peace, and integrity becomes clear. Imagine a different world where alienation and separativeness are understood; imagine children who are given a vision of what growing up can really mean. If they can see it, they'll know and grow.

I join many who cry into the wilderness: A new vision is needed for a regeneration of culture. The fulcrum of new generations will leverage the change.

What Is It To Really Grow Up?

Adult Preface
(Children can skip this.)

"What Is It To Really Grow Up?" is a six-week writing 'unit' (via a series of talks, prompts, and responses) I developed and engaged with children for over a quarter century. As the name suggests, this kid-accessible dialogue addresses the developmental process itself as well as personally developing new strengths. Both objectively and subjectively, it portrays a fully evolving spectrum, with detailed, affective-emphasis on understanding childhood and human responsibility.

Keeping it simple and connected to the natural world, the colors of the rainbow are correlated to the stages of life — and this spectrum is felt personally as "growing up" through the colors, hues, and stages of maturation.

After the participant takes note and records their responses to multiple facets of developmental challenges and abilities (filling in their **blank chart** — see the next page), they are then challenged to write a summary, weaving the horizontal, parallel threads in maturing progressions. By this understanding (and by example), there is an easy intertwining of multiple threads. One naturally exercises the writing technique of parallelism into a fabric of deep understanding.

At first (in this written form of my lectures), I explicitly insert suggestions for pauses, discussions, quick writes, and filling in the appropriate boxes on the chart, but soon leave that to the art of the teacher. By the end, all pertinent aspects of growing up are covered. See the **filled-in chart** at the end for full clarification.

Both children and adults need to have a full-spectrum understanding about what growing up could be. My fourth and fifth grade students in inner-city Richmond, San Francisco, and Pinole gave me reflections, suggestions, and gratitudes.
The vision of true maturity naturally inspires us to grow up from our earthen roots and rise into real adulthood. Standing firmly upon this beautiful world, we see how we can help.

My thanks goes out to the many kids over the last quarter-century who took these lessons to heart, and to the adults and parents who listened and contributed as well. More than the conglomeration of the good things I have heard, tried, and repeated because of impact or efficacy, these talks and exercises are a reflection of pedagogical features I learned in the ashram schools of Adidam, where I was both a growing student and a teacher of children. I shout eternal gratitudes to my beloved master-teacher, Adi Da Samraj—from whom I learned the fullness of love and education.

The Developmental Rainbow: Ready to be filled in...

A Kid's Guide to Growing Up	Color/Stage 1 Red Years	Color/Stage 2 Orange Years	Color/Stage 3 Yellow Years
STARTS (approximate years)			
FOCUS			
MATURES			
SAYS			
UNDERSTANDS THROUGH			
WEAKNESS			
UNHEALTHY IMAGE			
DISCIPLINE MAKES MOST SENSE			
IMAGE TEST			
MOOD			
IMAGE OF MATURITY			

For the kids:

Lots of people think that growing up stops when our body stops growing — when we're about 17 to 21 years of age. In fact, the word "adult" (ripe) comes out of the word "adolescent" (ripen); red apples ripen from green ones, adult comes after adolescent, yep. But being an "adult" means a lot more than flesh and bones, yes? We keep on growing as a person beyond the body fullness, eh? [Q&A/Discussion, onto board/projected]

At 18, we are considered an "adult" for many things, like driving freely, voting, joining the service, or college, and making a lot of our own decisions. Around 23, the brain stops growing. But just getting to be "big" or making our own decisions or even voting is not all that there is to being "grown-up". It's a lot more than that, so it is very useful to have a clear idea of what really grown-up could be. What do you think 'grown up' means, or should mean? [Discussion, sharing, and notes.]
`

Well, there are many, many ways we could talk about the phases of growing up and all of these descriptions are helpful. Almost every culture, people, religion, and philosophy has a way of talking about growing up. It's like talking about the stages of a plant — like an apple tree: if we start with the seed, then it sprouts, it grows into a sapling, and when it's big enough for blossoms, it makes apples with seeds. The seeds fall to the ground, the apple part makes the soil rich for the seeds and the cycle starts all over — and the tree grows bigger with every cycle for a while, lingers for a few years, and then passes. Now humans are a lot more diverse, complicated, and developed than apple trees; even still, we can talk about our stages of growing up.

Have you ever seen how a prism breaks clear light into the colors? We could look very, very closely and say that there are a hundred million colors in the spectrum, or we could step back and say that there are seven. In the same way, we could look very closely and find a hundred different hues of people growing up, but to be simple, we're going to mimic the "seven colors" of the rainbow and just talk about seven general stages of growing up, focusing almost entirely on the first three stages of childhood.

Letting each stage be associated with a traditional color of the rainbow, we'll ask questions at every stage/color. Four examples are: In each color of childhood, what are the strengths, challenges, understanding, and enjoyments?

RED

There are many phases in the first six years, just like there are many colors of red, but first let's talk about the red or first stage all together. The first stage of growing up, likened unto the color red, starts with the first breath and goes through the loss of the baby teeth at about 6 or 7 years of age. [Fill in the relevant boxes on the chart as we progress.] The red stage is focused in the body and being autonomous in the body. We learn to walk and talk and pee and poo all by ourselves. More than that though, we learn to be all by ourselves, to be rested, to go to sleep by ourself, and although we are dependent on "grown-ups" and need to feel safe, we can do a lot of things "all by myself". What do you remember doing "all by yourself"? Write it down. (pause)When we're little, we don't just walk along, we jump over lines, we walk on lines, we skip, we play with trying new things and relearning old things. We delight in new experiences and getting good at doing things. We are focused in growing.

We learn about and feel to others, of course, but the main focus is a healthy me, a rested sense. The first stager says, "I can do it." Who remembers saying that? What was it about? Write it down. (pause)

Because our body is the main focus, it is good if grown-ups don't talk too much when we mess up, but interact with us bodily: Hold us, move us away from bad situations. Some direct talk is good, but ideas are secondary to moving our bodies. We understand with our body more than talk, talk, talk. Who knows what I'm talking about?

In the first seven years, there is also an abundance of magic. From Fairy Tales to Santa Claus, from magic wands and spirits to fables, tales, and magical stories, we are enchanted by what we do not know and what we learn in the red years. We're learning, learning, learning. What were your favorites stories, parables, and myths when you were little? Why? If you had a new friend who had never heard of your favorite myth or story, what would you tell them? Find a partner and tell them your story,

pretending they've never heard of it. [Follow this by having them write it down.]

Most first stagers really like sweets — foods are a big focus for the red body and mind. But red sweetness can be sticky. The unhealthy side of the body-focused person makes for sugarized, couch potatoes and screen-entranced eyes. Our challenge is to not get dull. As we mature in the first years, we learn to discipline unhealthy eating, and not watch too much screens and do lots of things with your body. Do you have limits on screens? We've got to move and play and look and see. Where do you go outside for natural surroundings? What do you like to do outside? What is it like for you in nature? Write your answer to these question. (pause)

Starting about age four, a first stager can learn to take a big breath in hard times. We can always take a big breath to feel better, even if we're feeling pretty good. Try it now, take a long breath, feeling to natural happiness.

We learn to use our breath to focus. For me, learning to tie my shoelaces was very hard. I remember the exact moment I tied my shoes (I never had to ask mean Ronnie Carter again) and jumped high into the air. What do you remember trying very hard at when you were little? Write it, tell me all about it. [pause, re-punctuate the story necessities of when, where, what, who...why]

As we complete and brighten the red years (about 6-7 years old), we run peacefully down the path and don't always have to be looking back at Mom and Dad to make sure we are OK. There is still a mood of being dependent on them, of course, but we can rest without them and we can do it. Tell me your story about being away from your caretakers and how you could rest, feel peace.

ORANGE

When we start losing our "baby" teeth, the second great stage of childhood begins to emerge. New feelings and energies run through you as orange blossoms from the red years. To the depth we have

learned to rest, we learn to let our feeling "fly". Music is great, beauty is great, and harmonies of all kinds are great to the energetic feelings and flying orange mind. What were you into when you were eight or nine or ten? Why did you like it so? Did you get good at it? Ever do it tooo much? What things did you learn from it?

Second stage kids still love food and are enchanted by the seasons, but in addition to simple pleasures, we are working with feelings, like how we seem to others and who likes us. Everyone wants to be included. Of course, but this is huge in the orange period.
In the orange years, it is important not just to feel included, but to learn to include more and more people and things in our feelings. We learn that best way to feel included is to practice including others. (It's not easy and we get our feelings hurt sometimes.) Do you remember a time when you were the new kid? I think everyone has a memory of trying to be someone's friend but getting our feelings hurt; do you?

Another way of saying 'being included' is 'belonging'. (We belong where we can let our feelings go.) Friends and family and groups and village-community feel important, and you are right; belonging is important, feeling included is important. Who can tell me a time when you felt included. When, Who, Where, What...

Orange kids, like red ones, remain in a mood of dependence on others. In the second seven years, we are dependent on membership and being-included. We need to feel a sense of belonging all of our life. Write down the names of one or two friends, your family names, your neighborhood, city, state, country, continent, your planet. You are a part of your church, mosque, temple, class in school, or favorite park.

Learning about belonging is good, because we really are connected to others and the world around us, even when we're feeling alone. Did you know that humans are a single family? We all have the same great-great-great-great-great-great-great-great-10,000-great-grandmother. Do you have a cousin who is a bit weird, but you love them anyway? It's really true, we are a very big family. Hey cuz! Since everyone here is basically your cousin, what does that make you think? (Long discussion/sharing)

In the orange feeling of connectedness, we can feel and see how everything is connected to everything else. The more we act and behave with the sense of connectedness (like with friends and family), the better we feel and the better we all are. Are you still a good help around the house? Can you tell me about a recent time of sharing? What does "forgive" mean to you? Who makes you laugh?

Where a first stager says, "I can do it," the second stager expresses, "I feel, I am." Let your feeling go and say to yourself, "I am." Or "I am your friend."
In these learning-to-feel years, we experiment with feelings and ways of acting by remembering someone else and acting like them; it is good to have role-models we can look up to in the orange years. Who are some of your role models and what do you like about each one?

When we are strong in the orange ways, we can hold onto others in our feeling, and we can also let go. We exercise our new feeling-wings by letting go to music; by listening, playing, or dancing. Or we invest ourselves in performances, or letting the body go in all kinds of ways, like sports and arts. It helps to build your focus, for sure, but everyone also experiences 'letting-go' and being 'in the zone', at least for a little while. In ancient times, they called that "being taken by the muse". It's focus and letting-go both together: like in Muse-ik...
We learn to flow, dance, and soar. What do you like to do where you really let go? Give me an example, how you felt, what you learned.
What is some of your favorite music? What song or game or hobby were you really into in the orange years that you did a lot? Who turned you on to it? Ever get 'in the zone', where everything went perfectly? How did that feel? Where were you? What were you doing?

We learn to flow, dance, and soar. What do you like to do where you really let go and you get into 'the zone'? Dance? Singing? Instruments? Drawing? Athletics? Give me an example, how you felt, what you learned.

We are strong in the orange years when we are strong in our "letting go" strength. We let go to good feelings found in music, the arts, sports,

family, and friends. But also we learn to let go of bad feelings (aka "forgiveness" of ourselves and others).

The exploration of feelings is not always pleasant in the orange years. Sometimes we feel weird or even bad for no reason at all, or we'll think someone doesn't like us when they really do. When a new feeling emerges, it can be very awkward and even a bit painful or scary, or weird like a baby bird cracking out of its shell. Is is important to learn to recognize and talk about emotions, both in yourself and in others. Any one here ever use a diary? Can you picture in your mind some new-feeling that was hard or strange? (Alt.) Can you write about feelings that are sometimes hard to talk about?

It is good to remember that growing pains and weird feelings have a way of becoming wonderful pleasures and true strengths later. If we can't let our feelings go, we work on strengthening our letting-go-wings. It is important to practice letting go in all kinds of ways. Can you remember a time when you felt really awkward around other people? Did you let it go later? Tell me.

Because membership is so important to the feelings of second stagers and society, there are many stories that share about the far-reaching effects of harmonious and disharmonious behavior. For example, there are many stories all around the world about what Western people call "the golden rule" — treating others like you want to be treated, 'what goes around, comes around'. In India, it is called "karma". The grown-up fancy word for this is "reciprocity". Write it down.
Stories really help the second stager to understand this relationship between how we act and what happens. In stories, it is often a bad guy that gets what he deserves, right? In ancient China it was said, "Your thoughts go out a thousand miles, how far do you think your actions go?" What is the first story that comes into your mind where what happens is connected with how someone felt and acted? Have you ever seen this in real life?

The hardest test in the orange years is to not reject others, even when we feel rejected. We fail at this a lot, but we keep forgiving and trying — and we get stronger. We learn to forgive others and know our apologies help. We want to be forgiven too. We do it already, but

forgiveness is a like a muscle we need to exercise. Can you write about a time when you said "I'm sorry", and follow this story with one where you forgave someone?

Teasing (within the feeling of inclusion) can be fun and happy, but teasing can be mean in the orange years, because it feels like we are being threatened with exclusion. Do you remember a time when someone was mean to you? Do you know how teasing can be fun and loving?

It's hard to remember, but people who are weak in letting go and don't feel good inside, they feel bad and small, and sometimes they put other people down, just so that they can feel big. They are just unhappy and don't know how to get happy. This happens to everybody: we feel bad and then we act poorly and make matters worse. Have you ever seen anybody teased in a mean way? Has it ever happened to you?

But as we grow strong in the orange years, our powers of letting go and of inclusion grow. Intelligently including-others relieves us of feeling rejected in a very positive way. Even our teasing feels loving and friendly. We learn to include others more and more and we are likewise included. Can you recall a time when someone made you feel included? Can you also recall a time when you reached out to someone new or alone?

In the orange time, we feel how we are a unique energy or person or spirit. And because we are sensitive to energy and feelings, we learn to see the energy or spirit or person in others, rather than their clothes or skin color (and even beyond their hurts). I like to say, "It is way more important how you see than how you look." [Discussion]
Have you ever heard the expression "the eyes are windows to the soul"? Can you tell me a time when you looked at the deeper feeling or soul of someone instead of their clothes or facial features?

Like everyone, we don't want to be measured by our skin color or hair shape or disabilities, but by our presence or spirit, and by our trust-ability. Can you remember a time when you were misjudged because of the way you looked? Tell me the whole story.

Back in the red years, a little kid could run naked on the beach and nobody cared. But in the elementary years, naked is more private, and boyhood

and girlhood take on a new depth and complexion. It is often confusing, feeling weird and new things, right? And there are many roles that we can play out. For example, when boys are learning to be boys and girls are learning to be girls, some go through a phase where, in order to define their own gender feeling, they reject the other gender as some form of "yuk-ee". Did you ever think boys or girls (or anything in-between) were yukky?

If we do like someone, we may keep it a secret. Did you ever like someone and keep it a secret?

Agreements are important to the orange mind of the second stager. Orange kids like agreements: agreements about games, expectations, promises, and all sorts of energy exchanges. Agreements are a form of feeling-energy, which is the main focus for the elementary years. For 'orange kids', it is easier for them to keep an agreement than just do what they are told. Agreements make sense to the second stager. What kind of agreements do you have at home?

We need to be passionate and daydream especially in the orange years, but the challenge is working to stay in harmony with those around us. Especially in orange, we often feel passionate about many things, or one thing, and sometimes we are so over-focused in our passion that we exclude others in an un-feeling way. Or instead of passionate action, we may give ourself up to dreaminess, and likewise forget about others. Learning to keep others in our feelings is the challenge of the second stager. Do you remember a time where you were completely forgetting others by dreaminess? Or did your mother or brother ever call you and you couldn't hear them because you were too into something?

We no longer believe in Santa Claus the way a four year old would, but we really love stories and understand that myths have meaning. In the maturation of the second stage, we can listen to a myth "as if" it were true. A kid once commented to me, "Myths are false on the outside, but true on the inside." That's it. What did the myth make you think of? Why did someone repeat that story? What was a lesson you could get from a story?

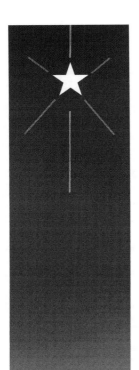

Instead of forgetting others, we learn to exercise the flower of feeling: we may reach out to another, play actively, or trust quietly. We notice how our breath focuses our feelings and we feel a blossoming feeling. Focused in good feeling, we take a breath; riding our spirited breath, we are inspired. We hold our focus and thus we soar with confidence. We breathe the wind of the Earth's breath, or we blow and burn with feeling — in music or dance, or any of the arts, or in the excellence of athletics. We must remember to use our breath both in times of stress (a-spiring for relief) and fullness (in-spired). Can you remember a couple of times where your breath was useful to your focus and feeling?

YELLOW:
Biological signs of puberty may appear before the fullness of the orange years because the stages overlap. In the fullness of orange, yellow can be seen. Sometime after puberty starts and the feeling years blossom, the last stage of childhood begins. At first gender and sex-talk can be embarrassing for many people, but "growing up" is the topic here.
In the yellow years, puberty supercharges our growth and things change. In their bodies, boys make seed and girls make their eggs regularly available — and a great force for making kids emerges. We are attracted to others in a new way. Puberty prepares the body for sexual intercourse, and the evolutionary urge to continue the species makes sexuality grow shinier and shinier, and suddenly some people are way more attractive to us. Sexuality is a big, growing force and learning possibility. Who has seen how sexiness is used to get your attention to sell stuff?

Yellow blossoms brightly from the orange patterns of energy-feeling, and we are a person in a new and deeper way. No longer is the focus only in body or feelings, in red and orange, but we come to our bright yellow mind in a new and powerful stance. Now, in addition to the body's sexy "shine" of reproductive possibility, the focus of brain development moves to the higher brain and the mind grows in power for ideas. In addition to tales and a storied understanding, there is a compelling logic. We understand the moral of the story. We get concepts, we are focused in conceiving patterns and relations in the forms and energies we experience.

Craftiness erupts from the storied-mind of the elementary years, as cunning/principles emerge from mythic feelings and simple pleasures. Concepts grasp the patterns in our perceptions.

You understand more deeply and can talk about the meaning of the story or the principle amongst the many. Who remembers suddenly "getting it", like when a old name suddenly had new meaning or you understood something deeper? [Alternative:. Consider the birth of Athena, the cunning one, as she bursts forth already mature from the forebrain of Zeus. The divinity of Athens is quite cunning, eh?]

Growing in yellow, we are based on our own rational assessment, even if incomplete. Via understanding, our capacity for intention is forged. Where the first stager says, "I can do it", and the second stage says, "I feel, I am", the third stager says, "I know, I will." Now we begin to be a young man or a young woman —and the teen years of "trial adulthood" begin. Write it down.

A teen doesn't do well with just doing what they're told, as if they were a first stager or red kid. And agreements are good only if they make sense to the teen. The yellow mind needs to be involved; the teen needs to understand and co-create his or her personal parameters of freedom and responsibility. If they understand a responsibility, it is much easier to exercise it. Just doing it because they're told to or because "it's good for you" doesn't cut it. What responsibilities do you have that you understand, and what freedoms do you appreciate?

As the third stage erupts, the feeling of dependence that dominated the first two stages fades, and independence becomes strong. But independence alone is not the solution to life and so the third stager oscillates between independence and dependence in a mood that is not shaped by dependence but with dilemma. Can you see the dilemma of wanting to go out on your own but having to ask for the car keys or money or help? Back and forth between dependence and independence forms the sensation of dilemma.

Dilemma and doubt riddle the conceptual mind of the adolescent. There's a whole lot of thinking going on! Sometimes doubt and dilemma are too strong and our spirit is depressed. Doubt, dilemma,

and depression make up a three-headed dragon of the yellow-mind years. Everybody has to deal with at least one set of monster teeth on the three-headed dragon: dilemma, doubt, depression. It is helpful to recognize the dragon when it comes upon you. The teenage years can be a very hard battle. And the dragon sometimes wins, who has heard of teen suicide?

The teen years can be the most difficult in life. Not only are we more distinct and individual than ever, we feel more separate from everyone and most things. Suddenly one day, we are as if behind our eyes in a chatterbox prison, looking out, thinking constantly and feeling strange and alone.

The hero's journey begins. Our sword must be sharp. And all the time, a forest of thinking, thinking, thinking. Does thinking ever drive you crazy?

It is good to know that this is normal, most people experience this. (And just like in the second stage, it's good to have faith and remember that what seems to be weak eventually becomes a power.) Isn't it great when you find out someone else is crazy just like you are? Write an entry about why you think it is important to know that this inside-the-head possession is a common experience.

This constant thinking is not quieted by a great thought! The chatterbox of mentality is slowly silenced by a power in the harmony of good living. The harmonic strength of good living makes a resonance in reality, and the overtones lead to a quietness. Every religion has a list of ways to live they consider harmonic. From the eight fold path to the ten commandments; from "nothing in excess" to Sokrates' wisdom, we find this restraint. What is your favorite understanding of temperance?

The teen-age years should be honored as a time of trial-adulthood where the kids demonstrate they understand the correlation between sometimes dangerous freedom and necessary responsibilities. If teens want liberties (ha ha), then they must assign responsibilities to preface and ground their freedoms. These arrangements of responsibility are created by the teen (in concert with caretakers/mentors). What freedoms do you want, and what kinds of responsibilities do you think would show you can handle extra freedoms? This could be three long lists, including also appropriate consequences for irresponsibilities (stated by the teen).

The third stage is complete when the will of the understanding person brings the body and feeling (evidenced by behavior) to a growing harmony. We certainly do not have to be perfect, maybe not even pretty good, but if we merely try, "for real" and consistent, anyone can learn to slowly 'tune' their life to harmony. Merely by remaining oriented to growth in feeling and attuning ones actions to harmony, the mature teen slowly emerges as a healthy, respectful, open, sharp, strong, and peaceful character. How can you grow more in these areas?

In attending to a harmonious life, higher brain-functions develop easily. Teens need to know this: the more harmony they can develop in their bodies, feelings, and behaviors, the cooler and greater the brain (and social connections) can become. Sexual feelings should be freely felt, of course, yet our sexual behavior remains restrained (whatever that means to you). Discipline is good for the brain (as well as the mind). Feeling sexual energies and applying intelligent restraints is like sending awesome energy up to our own private genius. It's called growing up for a reason. This idea of temperance and sexual temperance will change over time, but what do they mean to you now?

What you take into your body is important to your brain, and therefore, mind. Can you see how the laws about intoxicants carry wisdom? — for drugs mess with the higher brain functions. Therefore, teens should avoid intoxicants (and eat well) in respect for the very best their own brains have to offer. Every kind of life-supporting habit helps the brain — this is especially important in the teen years when the mind is so central. If the brain is healthy, the mind is more easily coherent. Experiment with how more fresh food and consistent exercise helps you see clearer. The mature teen understands all of this and then applies his or her will to slowly and firmly adapt to harmonious actions. This is intelligent living, where joy can grow beyond mere moments. Discuss what smart living means to you with a friend, then make notes of all the points that were covered. Compare notes and revise.

At first, when the teen is trying on the mantel of self-direction, she and he often asserts their will and does what she and he wants! In the beginning of yellow's independence, the teen turns to mechanisms in

the body and feeling in the pursuit of happiness. It is fun city, littered with occasional disasters. Have you ever gotten in trouble because you went too far?

But then comes the great moment in the yellow years when the person intentionally turns from merely exploiting the mechanisms of the nervous system to the happiness that is deeper than stimulation and self-satisfaction. We stretch our vision from superficial pleasures to long-term or deep happiness. We cut through the surface features of life and open up the depth of real living and true happiness. (Alt. Consider the story "Perseus, Medusa, and Pegasus" in Core Stories) Like Perseus, with adamant decisiveness and focused reflection, we build our energy and intention. Do you remember purposely choosing sharing or serving over selfishness?

This steady turn-about from short-term pleasures to long lasting happiness (from too-much self to the labor of relationship), is the sign of a great initiation into deeper self-understanding. Then the mature teen comes to understand Sokrates' dictum, "An unexamined life is not worth living". Growing in this commitment to self-understanding and willfully turning from self-concern to growing in love and service, we look beyond the superficial freedoms to include a deeper light and responsible adolescence ripens. Instead of partying, we celebrate. Our conversion is like the conversion of matter into energy; pleasures into spirited living.

When we are strong in not re-acting like we did when we were little and are usually able to respond instead of react, the transcendence of childhood grows sufficient, and the uncommon maturation of true adulthood begins.

Consider the difference between responding and re-acting, between response-ability and drama. Rehearsal or present?

What have you learned and want to remember? How do we become strong in choosing longer-lasting happiness?

*****

That is the **conclusion** of the writing and learning about regular growing up. Have a long Q&A. **Review** the filled-out chart at the end.

In the Q&A, questions about the rest of the colors come up. Tell them you will answer them later. When all other review and questions are done, let them know that following address to the other colors is like a poem, suggestive rather than "fact" and they should just follow the ideas like a poem. What other wisdoms does it remind you of?

Write: (2-4 days) With the full chart in hand and taking all your notes and all your personalizations, write a full **summary** using the technique of **parallelism**. "In the red years, one is all about the body, while in the orange years...." See student sample.

*****

Brief notes on the upper colors:

Real adulthood begins as thinking slowly calms in thanking and the mind gives way to love. This naturalness, gratitude, and love is not mere sentiment, not the feelings of soaring emotion, nor is it riddled with the sense of romance, the promise of fulfillment or poignant angst. Real love is more like self-giving than self-soaring, more trusting than knowing, more thankful than thinking, more wounded than hurt. To love with depth is to serve and give beyond self-position. It is not self-emptying, like we have no needs, but it is self-giving, since we are grounded in self-knowledge and in touch with fullness. It is better to give than to receive, explained the Master of the Christians. This phase of self-giving and service is not just another seven year cycle. It is a lifetime of work and pleasure. Blessed are those who can serve.

If we keep growing, we become better and better at giving — and giving ourself up — and in that heart-giving, we rest, deeply. A resonant harmony is felt and seen in the interrelations with everything. In this "green" mind and light, all of life is felt and understood to be connected, interconnected, and integrated. The systems of everything are appreciated in a growing unity. Our mood of service naturally extends farther and farther. The world needs more green now.

There are colors above green, but few grow there. It takes a lifetime of harmonizing our life, greening our feeling, and practicing service to others. But if we persist in continual growth, wise decisions, committed

service, and deepening self-knowledge, we may emerge in uncommon wonder.

We deeply recognize an enlightened person; a sage, a savior, a prophet, an avatar, and see the incarnation of love. This example and imprint can give us inspiration and rest in the harmony of everything and the disharmonies in life. We let our mind fall into the heart, falling in love's bliss, breath after breath. In deep gratitude for the gifts of light, raptures of joy begin the blue upper worlds. We are admitted to the chambers of the heart, following the footsteps of sacred heroes. Seeing and feeling the wonders of open secrets, we learn to let loose in grateful simplicity and purity of joy — as the sky of mind turns from blue to indigo.

Now we see everything from pain and urge to highest light and deepest joy. We go down to the red animal and rise with celestial wings, and bring both the dog and angel to the heart. Fallen in fullness, melted through intimacy, we rest in reality's brightness, in the calm awareness of everything. Free-feeling-awareness witnesses all, letting all, being lived and lighted. We see that reality itself is a form of light and universal sentience, which shines out of every eye and dances in everything, as everything. All is consumed in a silent and thunderous I am.

In that deep violet sky, a star of clear light can readily be seen beyond the rainbow, the brilliant source of every color. $E = mc^2$ and everything from red dirt to solar cores and from sensation to sentience is made of conscious light.

*****

We can grow out of childish immaturities and adolescent disharmony into deep happiness and stable loving. We can. We can turn from brief pleasures to longer lasting ones. We're a fool if we don't. It's not the hokey-pokey, it's turning yourself about. It's not about being right or winning or achieving, but growing and turning or yielding into the "light". The steady presence of deepest reality always blesses us.

****

Here's a challenge for the teens: Go to the adults in your life who care for you and tell them you understand that teen years are a kind of "trial adulthood". Tell them you would like to consider all the freedoms you should have and what responsibilities you could assume to show the rightness of those freedoms. Tell your (parents) you would like to co-create all the responsibilities, freedoms, and consequences. If there is any disagreement, agree on who the arbiter will be. Clarity helps so much.

A Kid's Guide to Growing Up	Color/Stage 1 Red Years	Color/Stage 2 Orange Years	Color/Stage 3 Yellow Years
STARTS (approximate years)	with the first breath (0-7)	with the first permanent teeth (6-12)	with puberty and a plethora of ideas (12-21)
FOCUS	Body	Feelings. Sensitive to energies	Mind, and the consequent Will
MATURES	simple autonomy: pee, poo, dress, go to sleep, etc., "all by myself"	flying feelings, really lets go; "don't underrate, appreciate"	by turning from too much self to greater happiness
SAYS	"I Can do it!"	"I feel, therefore I am."	"I understand, I Will."
UNDERSTANDS THROUGH	Magic, Fairy Tales, Stories	Myths, Parables, precepts	Ideas, patterns, concepts
WEAKNESS	dull, sticky, dark red, spoiled	excluding others (too into something/ excessive daydreaming)	lost in a forest of thinking, thinking
UNHEALTHY IMAGE	Couch potato	rejecting others because you feel rejected	**3 Headed Dragon** of Dilemma, Doubt and Depression
DISCIPLINE MAKES MOST SENSE	directly telling, moving their bodies	agreements/ deals	by understanding, co-creating responsibilities and freedoms
IMAGE TEST	don't get dull	too obsessed/ can't rest	WILL you come to harmony?
MOOD	dependence	dependence	Dilemma (between independence and dependence)
IMAGE OF MATURITY	running down the path confidently, without <u>Mom</u> &	sensitive to others emotional fluency healthy role	Response-able and Open

Student Sample

Growing Up by Zoe, Fifth-Grade

Red Years

What does growing up really mean? Does it mean we have to stop watching Spongebob, or stop going downstairs for a midnight snack? No. We don't try to act different, it just happens. It means we are maturing.

But some things that growing up does mean is learning how to act responsible, making your own decisions, having freedom, and what most people are scared of, being independent. Like going off to college, it is your first time away from home and your family. That's your time to shine, and really feel like an adult.

Growing up can be thought of in many different ways, like an apple tree. It goes from a seed to a sprout, to a sapling, and next it starts flowering, and next it becomes a nice juicy apple with a good life that is until it gets eaten. Or you can say it's like: conception, womb, born, baby, infant, toddler, kids, grade school, preteen, teen, young adult, parenthood, old, dead.

But I am going to talk about it in the colors of the rainbow. For instance, the first color and phase is red, which is the cute, little innocent kid phase.

Red is basically from the first breath to when you start to loose your baby teeth. 1st stagers are always the ones who think anything is possible, therefore first stagers say, "I can do it." And since red is about being able to do anything, red is about the time when you can run down the path without your mom or dad.

But red does have weaknesses. 1st stagers' weaknesses are that they are most to be known as couch potatoes, or unhealthy. Red can be thought of as sticky or sweet. Kind of like a day when you veg on food and watch TV, that's like going back to red. So their test is to not get dull or bored.

For youngsters or "red" people, discipline is pretty easy for the parent. Instead of agreements or making a deal, parents direct their first stager's body into timeout or wherever their punishment spot is.

Since pre-schoolers are so devoted to doing things on their own, their basics are learning to do simple things like dress, pee, poop, and sleep by themselves.
But the last and final stage of red is magic. Which is a big part of red. Mostly because they are too young and gullible to understand. That is why younger kids believe in Santa Claus, toothfairie, monsters under your bed, etc... But as red slowly emerges to orange we continue....

Orange Years

Feelings, feelings, feelings... you know what that means, Orange! Orange is all about feelings and emotions as red is about body. Orange is about when you lose all your baby teeth and red is when you get them. But 2nd stage is also about getting new feelings, and learning how to work them. Like a new machine, it is fun to work with it and figure it out.

It's when you can keep your feelings in or let them fly, when you can let them go in other words. When you can really put your feelins out there, and take it all the way and not just half way. For example, you may tell somebody that you kinda like, but when your feelings fly you can say I really, really love you!

Orange is not too much different than red, but as reds are more into mimicking, orange people are into having role models. Even if you don't notice it, you do have role models.

If you are following the latest trends then that is considered a rolemodel. Another thing that is different is that 1st stagers can be directed into punishment, oranges have agreement/deals. IF you want a 2nd stager to do something the best way to handle it is with an agreement, like if your parent want you to do the dishes, oranges would want a reward.

The weakness of orange, though, can be pretty annoying to friends of the second stagers. Grade-schoolers tend to be the ones who really get into something. But that is not the best thing, because second stagers start excluding others for things like daydreaming, video games, computer games, etc....

But all of those things are just a spec on my shoulder, the big kahuna is learning not to reject others when you feel rejected. When all of your feelings are flying and free, it seems that when somebody puts you down, your first instinct is to do what they did to you.

Yellow years

Freedom! When a teen gets a hold of it, there's no stopping them. What do you think the first thing in their mind is, partying!! They exploit themselves. But I don't blame any teenager for wanting to have fun.

Yellow starts with puberty, where orange starts with toothfairie, and red starts with first breath. But yellow is about mind/will, because as you get older mostly everythinhg is based on your mind, but even some adults tstill have a little bit of the red/body phase in them.

Yellow may be the most unhealthy stage of the three, simply because of something known as the 3 headed dragon. Dilemma, doubt, and depression. Dilemma, which means can't decide between two things, can be a big part of yellow. For example, the subject of going to college is a good way to explain it. You may not be sure if you want to go far away or close to home. For instance, my brother decided to go somewhere far like San Diego State, but he ended up moving back. Yellow can be confusing!

But then comes the great moment, when you turn from self to great happiness. OK, say you find three pieces of candy. You might want to eat them all yourself, but yellow is when you can turn from just yourself to others also. Which may be thought of as trial adulthood.

3rd stagers say "I understand, I will," while 2nd stagers say, "I feel, therefore I am," as 1st stagers say, "I can do it." But to me, what the 3rd stager say I is most important, only because it really means something. Like if your family is having trouble, a yellow person would notice and say, "I understand" and help, because they are starting to get an adult mind.

Now when you get to yellow, it seems you are already co-creating your own life. You can say, "Mom, I think I should go to the party," instead of "momma, can I?" But the last part of yellow is ideas instead of myths or magic when you get the idea of something like Christmas instead of just knowing it's a myth.

*****

Thanks Zoe! Great Work

Unit Seven: Service Heroes

Integrating Research, Art, Poetry, and Taking Character

Common Core Standards Addressed

<u>Writing</u> **2a, b, e, 4, 6, 7**

Thanks for RVSD's Julia Wolcott and Julie Gallagher

Service Heroes—Biography Report

Objectives:

Over a few weeks, students will be reading a biography of a person who has made a positive contribution to our world. These are the "Service Heroes and Heroines" who have given of themselves, who understood the value of service and made a difference.

Samples are:

Martin Luther King, Jr.	John Muir	Alice Eastwood
Ben Franklin	Aung Sung Suu Ky	Caesar Chavez
Henry David Thoreau	Thomas Jefferson	Kong-Qiu
Helen Keller	Luther Burbank	Mahatma Ghandi
Greta Thunberg	Jane Goodall	Susan B Anthony
plus _____ (add your favorites)	plus _____	(local and familial heroes)

Students will report on their reading in a number of ways:

1. Completion of Biography Questionnaire–see handout
2. Biography Montage
3. Bio Poem
4. Theatrically Conduct an Interview <u>as</u> the person to the whole class – see handout

Teachers should calendar the following:

Activity	Approximate due date
Library/Computer Lab Visit/Choose Books	Week 1
Begin Questionnaire	Week 1
Intro Bio Poem	Week 1
Bio Poem and Montage Due	End of Week 2
Intro Interview	Week 3
Interview Due	End of Week 3

Biography Montage

Mon-tage n. the art or process of making a picture by bringing together into a single composition a number of different pictures so that they form a blended whole while remaining distinct.

Based on the above definition of montage, a biographical montage is an art composition that will blend pictures, photographs, and images from an individual's lifetime into a whole piece that will give the viewer a feel for the life and times of this particular individual. For example, if the individual lived a hard life of poverty difficulty, and sadness during the Depression, then the montage would have a theme of poverty, difficulty or sadness, reflecting that time. If the individual were an environmentalist, the montage would depict perhaps an outdoor theme combined with images of the individual's life.

Biography Montage Creation
Overview

- The montage is to be composed on a 8.5 x 17 piece of tag board, poster board, or any large paper.
- The montage will show the life and times of a biographical figure
- No "empty" space allowed
- The student's name, class, period and date will be on the back of the montage
- A list of at least three internet sources will be included on the back of the montage

Steps to Completion of Montage

1. Collect images

First, determine when this individual lived. What was going on in the world at that time? What was going on in this person's life? You will need to gather pictures and images from this individual's childhood into adulthood. Enlarge and shrink photos to allow yourself some freedom with step two. You will be given computer time to research, locate, and print images for your montage. You will record website data for your bibliography.

2. Arrange Images

Once you have printed and copied more than enough to fill a page, it is time to arrange the images in a way that will allow the viewer to get a feel for the life and times of this individual. BE sure to trim away excess details and backgrounds if they're not relevant; pay attention to where the eye will be drawn, is this what you want the viewer to focus on?

Finally, try different arrangements of your images on the paper before you decide to glue them down. Your images do not need to be the same size, angle, direction, or color.

3. Add color or Texture

Creativity comes in here. Which black and white images say the most about the life and times of your individual? How will you make these images stand out? Experiment with markers, colored pencils, watercolors; perhaps you could add some texture to the background of these images using colored paper, tissue, paints, etc.

When you have experimented with your images and textures and have decided on your final montage, glue everything onto the tag board.

4. Bibliography

A bibliography will accompany your montage (on the back). You will receive the proper format for the bibliography from your teacher.

Pre-Write for BioPoem

Line 1. **First name** _____

Line 2. One key adjective _____

Line 3. Sister (or brother, or wife) of _____

Line 4. Lover of (name three things) _____

_____   _____

Line 5. Who feels (three things)_____

_____   _____

Line 6. Who needs (three things)_____

_____   _____

Line 7. Who gives (three things) _____

_____   _____

Line 8. Who fears (three things) _____

_____   _____

Line 9. Who would like to see (three things)_____

_____   _____

Line 10. Resident of _____

Line 11. **Last name**_____

Student Samples:

Orville
Very gregarious
Proud of family: Wilber, Reuchlin, Katharing, Susan
Admirer of flight, family, inventions
Who felt proud, exhilarated, and lifted
Overcame gravity, poverty, and death of brother
Feared disappointment, failure, and death
Controlled powered flight
Lived on Hawthorn Street in Daytona, Ohio
Wright

Julius
Ruler
Son of Gaius
Admirer of his army, Pompey, power
Who felt he deserved to be dictator, felt defenseless because of his enemies,
And had a love for Cleopatra
Who overcame Gaul, Pompey's troops, and Egypt
Who gave us the history of his battles, the Roman calendar,
And gave his life for Rome
Who feared Pompey, his enemies, plots against him
Who was the emperor of Rome, a writer of history, and a military genius
Citizen of Rome
Caesar

Poem must be typed, edited for spelling errors, and begin and end with the names in italics.

Name: _____

Date: _____

TOPIC	KEY WORDS	BIBLIOGRAPHY INFO
Location/Places (Where did your person grow up, what cities, countries, did they live in? Other important places in his/her life?)		Website Title: http:// Website Title: http://
Time/Historical Events (What years did your author live? Were there major historical events that happened during his/her life?)		Website Title: http:// Website Title: http://
People (If your person is well-known, search for their image. Are there other well known people in your person's life?)		Website Title: http:// Website Title: http://
Objects (Are there any items that were significant in the life of your person? Objects that are needed for their job?)		Website Title: http:// Website Title: http://
Theme (What are big ideas/concepts that take place during your person's life? Poverty? The great outdoors? Animals?)		Website Title: http:// Website Title: http:// Website Title:
Other (Any other important images/ideas you would like to include in your montage.)		Title: http:// Website Title: http://

Biography Information Chart

Biography Interview: Taking Character

For the last portion of your Biography Book Report, you will be interviewed **as if you were the character** you are investigating. In order to help you take on the persona of your biography figure, you will **bring one prop** that represents your character. For example, if your biography figure is Jackie Robinson, you might bring a baseball bat, or if your biography figure is Jane Goodall, you might bring a pair of binoculars.

The student/character will answer a minimum of ten questions. These first five questions listed below are **mandatory**.

1.   When were you born?

2.   Describe your childhood.

3.   What were some of the major influences of your life?

4.   What are you most proud of?

5.   Describe a memory of your life that has special meaning for you.

 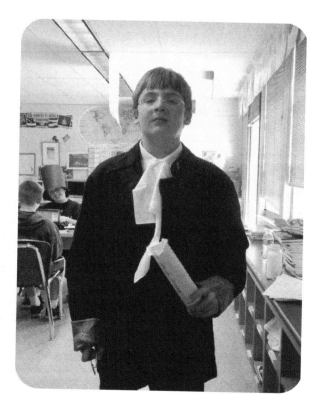

Taking it Home

WRITE: How Can I Serve? Challenge the students to imagine ways that they can serve and help the world, their neighborhood, and their family. Have them tell you what and how and why as well as hopes, fears, and visions.

"Deep happy is how my teacher understands me and makes learning fun."

APPENDICES

USA Common Core Educational Standards Addressed

An Introduction to Integral Theory

Whole Body Integration

Index

About the Author

The USA Common Core Educational Standards
(Grade 5, adjusted for California)

WRITING STANDARDS COVERED HEREIN

Text Types and Purposes

1. Write opinion pieces on topics or texts, supporting a point of view with reasons and information.

a. Introduce a topic or text clearly, state an opinion, and create an organizational structure
in which ideas are logically grouped to support the writer's purpose.

b. Provide logically ordered reasons that are supported by facts and details.

c. Link opinion and reasons using words, phrases, and clauses (e.g., consequently, specifically).

d. Provide a concluding statement or section related to the opinion presented.

2. Write informative/explanatory texts to examine a topic and convey ideas and information clearly.

a. Introduce a topic clearly, provide a general observation and focus, and group related
information logically; include formatting (e.g., headings), illustrations, and multimedia when useful to aiding comprehension.

b. Develop the topic with facts, definitions, concrete details, quotations, or other information and examples related to the topic.

c. Link ideas within and across categories of information using words, phrases, and clauses (e.g., in contrast, especially).

d. Use precise language and domain-specific vocabulary to inform about or explain the topic.

e. Provide a concluding statement or section related to the information or explanation presented.

3. Write narratives to develop real or imagined experiences or events using effective technique, descriptive details, and clear event sequences.

a. Orient the reader by establishing a situation and introducing a narrator and/or characters; organize an event sequence that unfolds naturally.

b. Use narrative techniques, such as dialogue, description, and pacing, to develop experiences and events or show the responses of characters to situations.

c. Use a variety of transitional words, phrases, and clauses to manage the sequence of events.

d. Use concrete words and phrases and sensory details to convey experiences and events precisely.

e. Provide a conclusion that follows from the narrated experiences or events.

Production and Distribution of Writing

4. Produce clear and coherent writing (including multiple-paragraph texts) in which the development and organization are appropriate to task, purpose, and audience. (Grade-specific expectations for writing types are defined in standards 1–3 above.)

5. With guidance and support from peers and adults, develop and strengthen writing as needed by planning, revising, editing, rewriting, or trying a new approach. (Editing for conventions should demonstrate command of Language standards 1–3 up to and including grade 5.)

6. With some guidance and support from adults, use technology, including the Internet, to produce and publish writing as well as to interact and collaborate with others; demonstrate sufficient command of keyboarding skills to type a minimum of two pages in a single sitting.

Research to Build and Present Knowledge

7. Conduct short research projects that use several sources to build knowledge through investigation of different aspects of a topic.

8. Recall relevant information from experiences or gather relevant information from print and digital sources; summarize or paraphrase information in notes and finished work, and provide a list of sources.

9. Draw evidence from literary or informational texts to support analysis, reflection, and research.

a. Apply grade 5 Reading standards to literature (e.g., "Compare and contrast two or more characters, settings, or events in a story or a drama, drawing on specific details in the text [e.g., how characters interact]").

b. Apply grade 5 Reading standards to informational texts (e.g., "Explain how an author uses reasons and evidence to support particular points in a text, identifying which reasons and evidence support which point[s]").

Range of Writing

10. Write routinely over extended time frames (time for research, reflection, and revision) and shorter time frames (a single sitting or a day or two) for a range of discipline-specific tasks, purposes, and audiences.

READING
Key Ideas and Details

1. Quote accurately from a text when explaining what the text says explicitly and when drawing inferences from the text.

2. Determine a theme of a story, drama, or poem from details in the text, including how characters in a story or drama respond to challenges or how the speaker in a poem reflects upon a topic; summarize the text.

3. Compare and contrast two or more characters, settings, or events in a story or drama, drawing on specific details in the text (e.g., how characters interact).

Craft and Structure

4. Determine the meaning of words and phrases as they are used in a text, including figurative language such as metaphors and similes. (See grade 5 Language standards 4–6 for additional expectations.)

5. Explain how a series of chapters, scenes, or stanzas fits together to provide the overall structure of a particular story, drama, or poem.

6. Describe how a narrator's or speaker's point of view influences how events are described.

Integration of Knowledge and Ideas

7. Analyze how visual and multimedia elements contribute to the meaning, tone, or beauty of a text (e.g., graphic novel, multimedia presentation of fiction, folktale, myth, poem).

8. (Not applicable to literature)

9. Compare and contrast stories in the same genre (e.g., mysteries and adventure stories) on their approaches to similar themes and topics.

Range of Reading and Level of Text Complexity

10. By the end of the year, read and comprehend literature, including stories, dramas, and poetry, at the high end of the grades 4–5 text complexity band independently and proficiently.

Reading Standards for Informational Text

Key Ideas and Details

1. Quote accurately from a text when explaining what the text says explicitly and when drawing inferences from the text.

2. Determine two or more main ideas of a text and explain how they are supported by key details; summarize the text.

3. Explain the relationships or interactions between two or more individuals, events, ideas, or concepts in a historical, scientific, or technical text based on specific information in the text.

Craft and Structure

4. Determine the meaning of general academic and domain-specific words and phrases in a text relevant to a grade 5 topic or subject area. (See grade 5 Language standards 4–6 for additional expectations.)

5. Compare and contrast the overall structure (e.g., chronology, comparison, cause/effect, problem/solution) of events, ideas, concepts, or information in two or more texts.

6. Analyze multiple accounts of the same event or topic, noting important similarities and differences in the point of view they represent.

Integration of Knowledge and Ideas

7. Draw on information from multiple print or digital sources, demonstrating the ability to locate an answer to a question quickly or to solve a problem efficiently.

8. Explain how an author uses reasons and evidence to support particular points in a text, identifying which reasons and evidence support which point(s).

9. Integrate information from several texts on the same topic in order to write or speak about the subject knowledgeably. (e.g., graphic novel, multimedia presentation of fiction, folktale, myth, poem).

8. (Not applicable to literature)

9. Compare and contrast stories in the same genre (e.g., mysteries and adventure stories) on their approaches to similar themes and topics.

Range of Reading and Level of Text Complexity

10. By the end of the year, read and comprehend informational texts, including history/social studies, science, and technical texts, at the high end of the grades 4–5 text complexity band independently and proficiently.

Reading Standards: Foundational Skills

Phonics and Word Recognition

3. Know and apply grade-level phonics and word analysis skills in decoding words.

a. Use combined knowledge of all letter-sound correspondences, syllabication patterns, and morphology (e.g., roots and affixes) to read accurately unfamiliar multisyllabic words in context and out of context.

Fluency

4. Read with sufficient accuracy and fluency to support comprehension.

a. Read on-level text with purpose and understanding.

b. Read on-level prose and poetry orally with accuracy, appropriate rate, and expression on successive readings.

c. Use context to confirm or self-correct word recognition and understanding, rereading as necessary.

SPEAKING AND LISTENING

1. Engage effectively in a range of collaborative discussions, building on others' ideas and expressing their own clearly.

2. Summarize a written text read aloud or information presented in diverse media and formats, including visually, quantitatively, and orally.

4. Report on a topic or text or present an opinion, sequencingd ieas logically and using appropriate facts and relevant, descriptive details to support main ideas or themes; speak clearly at an understandable pace.

4b. Memorize and recite a poem or section of a speech or historical document using rate, expression, and gestures appropriate to the selection.

An Introduction to Integral Theory
(as it relates to education)

Prologue: The Widest Embrace

Imagine a reading or social studies curriculum for accelerating young minds in public schools which uses a pedagogy that addresses developmental differences based on acute observation of cognitive capacities, with an interplay full of Piaget's observations, Vygotski's linguistic sensitivity, and Skinner's rewards; one that takes into account Gardner's multiple intelligences, and all kinds of learning. Impressive, you might think, but what if this curriculum did not take into account socioeconomic profiles, or Lorenz's ethological imprintings, or gender issues, or Bronfenbrenner's full range of the ecological contextualizations wherein a young person may find meaning? And what if this cognitively brilliant curriculum called students to Maslow's authentic learning satisfaction, but presumed ideal cooperation between students and teachers as if his spectrum of need meant nothing? Worse yet, what if it failed to recognize the pluralism and diversity of understanding — and presumed a homogeneous school setting within a homogeneous nation of idealized standards such as those found in the *No Child Left Behind* legislation? Perhaps this curriculum would address some of the conscientious social concerns of the day in an idealistic gesture, but it probably would take a neutral or absent stance in any philosophical debate. Furthermore, imagine that the developmental philosophy that was the underpinnings of our conceived curriculum narrowly presumed humanistic ideals as the goal of life — as if to satisfy Karl Marx, Adam Smith, Sigmund Freud, B.F. Skinner, and Madison Avenue. This iconic curriculum, strong in cognitive tasks but weak in context and insensitive to economic, racial, and cultural divides would not meet the intelligence of our day. In other words, in educational psychology, philosophy, and pedagogy, we must be sensitive to a wide and deep range of issues, not just cognitive or democratic ones, and appreciate every educational system of thought within a fully nuanced and all-inclusive framework. Otherwise, we are left with traditional thinking that is far too narrow and pedestrian in its pedagogy and its sociology.

In ancient Rome, there were two kinds of education for the two classes of people: the free and the slaves. First was a liberal education (L. *artes liberales*, literally "arts of freedom") for the wealthy, free men, and standard, informational education for the poor, the slaves, and the women who needed functional schooling. In other words, we must take into account the lessons we have learned about a full-bodied and all-inclusive education or else we will narrow our focus and give only the standard slave education to our children today. Indeed, it can be argued that this is what is happening. On the negative side of approaches such as the 2002 *No Child Left Behind* legislation, it can be said that we are dispensing only slave education to all. Except to rich, generally white families in private schools, or public schools that are voluntarily endowed.

But what if we brought a fully developed view to education, a view that embraced every previous philosophical, psychological, and pedagogical approach? Such a view would necessarily satisfy standards-based requirements (for slave education is subsumed by liberal education), and it would be adroitly sensitive to ecological context, gender, racial, and social-economic forces. In addition, the widest embrace would be politically active, culturally sophisticated, and neurologically aware. Lastly, a fully inclusive approach should have an attractive developmental invitation and spectrum that included every theorist from James Baldwin, John Dewey, and Jean Piaget to Sri Aurobindo, Plato, and Plotinus; from Abraham Maslow, Erik Erickson, and Lawrence Kohlberg to the Vedas, Gotama Shakyamuni, and Avatara Adi Da.

Fortunately for us, the latter work of Ken Wilber (1995-present) with his Four Quadrant, All Levels (and "all lines, states, and types"— more on this later) embrace gives us exactly the kind of "scientific" or neutral, post-metaphysical framework wherein we can locate every previous system of thought. For Wilber's All Quadrant, All Levels (and all lines, types, and states—hereby referred to by the acronym AQAL, pronounced "ah-qwul") approach is not only personal and developmental, it is objective and practical — scientific, ecological, social and political, cultural and philosophical. It is applicable to essentially all fields of knowledge, subjective and objective, holding pre-modern certainties, modern logic, and post-modern relativisms in a post-postmodern or integral frame of appreciation. Its all-inclusive and non-reductionist approach emphasizes that all levels and facets of self-development, science, society, and nature be allowed, appreciated, and addressed. While intellectually challenging and tending toward dry abstraction, Wilber's integral approach is still able to hold divergent consensa, both scientific and religious appreciations, and both personal and collective logics as it illuminates both the interiors and exteriors of many levels and perspectives in an integral, inclusive, and logical light. Wilber's historic work gives us this remarkable ability.

We might ask, "What does this do for us for real? Is this kind of talk merely ivory-tower eclecticism? If it is so useful, then how? Don't we have sufficient maps now?"

These are questions that must be asked (and will be addressed), but let me first offer a metaphor: It is possible to practice cartography from the prow of sailing ships and to come up with a sufficiently accurate map of the world to sail routinely from Venice to Benares. But the view from outer space not only crystallizes that view, it reveals systems, relationships, nuances, depth, and interplays that are only possible to see from another paradigm. Wilber's "Theory of Everything" is just the kind of meta-theory that give us the big picture wherein we can integrate all methodologies—giving us an "integral methodological pluralism". Thereby, we do not just allow a plurality of voices, but integrate them. With Wilber's models, we can exquisitely describe the features of the coastline, and we can see the contours of the whole earth...

[In the spirit of conservation and to read the full explication of these complex ideas, please go to the website: http://www.frankmarrero.com/ewExternalFiles/AQAL.pdf.]

Whole Body Integration

Right Brain
Art/Creativities

Left Brain
Academic Learning

Heart
Love, Praise, Appreciation, Applause, Feeling Breaths

Right Body
Active Body
Dance, Physical Education

Left Body
Calm Body
Yoga, TaiChi, Theatre

Whole Body Integration

Teaching only academic, 'left-brain' abstractions is an obvious focus in regular schooling, where state-demanded testing unduly pressures education. While this focus is very important, its partiality is actually harmful. If you hold a raisin close enough to your eye, you can block out the entire sun from your view. Academics are indeed very important, but the whole body is necessary for real education.

We need to balance and enlighten our necessary abstractions with art, music, exercise, and feeling. This is an artful process, for we need more than left-brained abstractions, we need the whole body. We must balance our academics with wholeness; we <u>can</u> integrate them all. So in addition to academic learning, always include artful representations of the subject matter, add theatre, and similar expressions.

Integrating multiple dimensions not only enhances learning, it serves the very being in wholeness. Keeping whole-body integration in mind, we can move through the quadrants of the body (as depicted in the chart on the previous page). For instance, we might start a class with full, calming breaths, imagining a scene and posing an inquiry. With this visualization as a basis, we investigate the inquiry with academic challenges and exercise our capacities for abstraction. We might conclude this with an art project or music or a dance or a dramatization—which will serve both the whole brain and the abstract learning. We might take a breath or few of appreciation or praise or applause. Then outside for athletics or play. Back in the class, we might first exercise calming and resting or gratitudes and feeling breaths before beginning a new cycle.

Of course, this is an ideal that does not always fit, but wholeness is not an idea we can discard. Indeed, wholeness is the fullness of real education.

闻而忘之；见而记之；行而知之

"I listen and I forget; I see and I remember; I do and I understand."

Index

About the Author

For over a quarter century, Frank Marrero taught in the San Francisco Bay area, from inner city public schools to private ashrams, from kindergarten helper to university lecturer. His focus all the while has been in developing curricula to nurture and develop affective strengths (including character education, emotional fluency, moral values, and self-awareness) in addition to academic rigor. His works have been lauded in superlatives by scholars, educators, parents, and children. He holds a Masters in the Arts of Teaching, and also taught in the Department of Religion and Philosophy at John F. Kennedy University.

Frank is the author of several books: *Lincoln Beachey:* The Man Who Owned the Sky, the definitive biography of the "Forgotten Father of Aerobatics"; *Recollections of Sokrates,* a novel about the last two months of the Sage of Athens; *The View from Delphi:* Rhapsodies on the Spiritual Foundations of Western Philosophy; *Deep Roots,* Illuminations in Etymology; *The Superpowers of Fasting,* Ancient Wisdom and Medical Miracles; *A Monkey's Tale for the Divine Person*, a book of leelas; and of course the companion volume to this text: *Core Stories. Nothing Makes Me Happy* is forthcoming.

Just inside the Dipylon Gates on the Way to the Agora
Athens, Hellas; October 2018

Frank is the proud parent of two bright and strong adults: Salem and Ella. Frank lives in celebration with his wife Marielle van Cann and her remarkable son Sem in The Netherlands.

To see all of his writings, please visit www.frankmarrero.com.

Hearty thanks flies to the many teachers who contributed, especially: Peter Churchill, Haniel Dufoe, Stephanie Samuels, Stephanie Eichleay, Alison Waldenberg, Sheila McBroom, Ann Diskin, Julie Galleger, and Julia Wolcott. Acknowledgements and gratitudes go to Judith Parkinson and Lydia DePole who furnished the not-credited illustrations. Appreciations to Marielle van Cann for her review and proofing of this text. Thanks to my students for their writing samples, their art work and their heart-work.

Gratitude most of all goes to my beloved teacher Adi Da, who suggested this curriculum and guided it. With joyous clarity, Adi Da taught me what education is at its best and what love feels like most fully.

Adi Da left, author right,
Tumomama Gorge, Kauai
September 9, 1982

Core Stories

Deep Myths, Wise Tales, and Biographies of Inspiration

Frank Marrero, M.A.T.
Enelysios

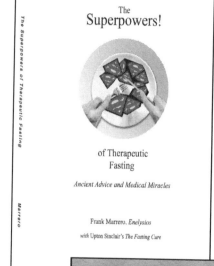

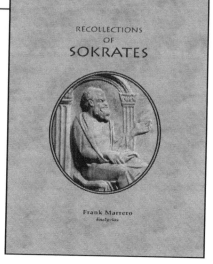

Made in the USA
San Bernardino, CA
09 August 2019